# THE ULTIMATE VALUES OF
# THE AMERICAN POPULATION

Volume 23, Sage Library of Social Research

1. **DAVID CAPLOVITZ**: The Merchants of Harlem: A Study of Small Business in a Black Community
2. **JAMES N. ROSENAU**: International Studies and the Social Sciences: Problems, Priorities and Prospects in the United States
3. **DOUGLAS E. ASHFORD**: Ideology and Participation
4. **PATRICK J. McGOWAN and HOWARD B. SHAPIRO**: The Comparative Study of Foreign Policy: A Survey of Scientific Findings
5. **GEORGE A. MALE**: The Struggle for Power: Who Controls the Schools in England and the United States
6. **RAYMOND TANTER**: Modelling and Managing International Conflicts: The Berlin Crises
7. **ANTHONY JAMES CATANESE**: Planners and Local Politics: Impossible Dreams
8. **JAMES RUSSELL PRESCOTT**: Economic Aspects of Public Housing
9. **F. PARKINSON**: Latin America, the Cold War, and the World Powers, 1945-1973: A Study in Diplomatic History
10. **ROBERT G. SMITH**: Ad Hoc Governments: Special Purpose Transportation Authorities in Britain and the United States
11. **RONALD GALLIMORE, JOAN WHITEHORN BOGGS, and CATHIE JORDAN**: Culture, Behavior and Education: A Study of Hawaiian-Americans
12. **HOWARD W. HALLMAN**: Neighborhood Government in a Metropolitan Setting
13. **RICHARD J. GELLES**: The Violent Home: A Study of Physical Agression Between Husbands and Wives
14. **JERRY L. WEAVER**: Conflict and Control in Health Care Administration
15. **GEBHARD LUDWIG SCHWEIGLER**: National Consciousness in Divided Germany
16. **JAMES T. CAREY**: Sociology and Public Affairs: The Chicago School
17. **EDWARD W. LEHMAN**: Coordinating Health Care: Explorations in Interorganizational Relations
18. **CHARLES G. BELL and CHARLES M. PRICE**: The First Term: A Study of Legislative Socialization
19. **CLAYTON P. ALDERFER and L. DAVE BROWN**: Learning from Changing: Organizational Diagnosis and Development
20. **L. EDWARD WELLS and GERALD MARWELL**: Self-Esteem: Its Conceptualization and Measurement
21. **ROBERT S. ROBINS**: Political Institutionalization and the Integration of Elites
22. **WILLIAM R. SCHONFELD**: Obedience and Revolt: French Behavior Toward Authority
23. **WILLIAM C. McCREADY with ANDREW M. GREELEY**: The Ultimate Values of the American Population

# The Ultimate Values of the American Population

**WILLIAM C. McCREADY**
with
**ANDREW M. GREELEY**

Volume 23
SAGE LIBRARY OF
SOCIAL RESEARCH

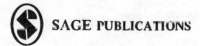 **SAGE PUBLICATIONS**     Beverly Hills     London

*For information address:*

SAGE PUBLICATIONS, INC.
275 South Beverly Drive
Beverly Hills, California 90212

SAGE PUBLICATIONS LTD
St George's House / 44 Hatton Garden
London EC1N 8ER

Printed in the United States of America

**Library of Congress Cataloging in Publication Data**

McCready, William C                1941—
    The ultimate values of the American population

    (Sage library of social research ; v. 23)
    Includes bibliographical references and index.
    1. United States—Religion—1945—    —Case studies.
2. Religion and sociology—Case studies.  3. Worth—
Case studies.  I.  Greeley, Andrew M., 1928—    joint
author.  II.    Title.
BR526.M28    200'.973        75-40337
ISBN 0-8039-0502-5
ISBN 0-8039-0503-3 pbk.

FIRST PRINTING

# TABLE OF CONTENTS

# LIST OF TABLES

*To Nancy*

*Chapter 1*

# INTRODUCTION

There can be little doubt that the subject of "religion" has been gaining in popularity in recent years. We hear about it on talk shows; we read about it as manifested in Jesus movements or meditation sects; and we can hardly help but notice the resurgence in interest in the occult, spiritism, mysticism, and other forms of other-worldly contact. The central question which this religious reawakening has posed for the discipline of sociology is contained in the secularization hypothesis. There are two parts to the puzzle: Is our society becoming more religious or less religious as time passes? And, given that we can come up with some viable answer to the first question, is it a good or a bad thing? These two questions have been responsible for putting the sociology of religion back into a central position in the discipline as a whole.[1]

Much of the controversy revolves around the various definitions of "religion" which are used. "Religion" can be limited to devotions such as attending religious services or recitation of specific prayers. It may also include adherence to certain doctrinal positions such as the Virgin Birth or the literal interpretation of the Bible. For some authors, notably Luckmann, there is really nothing in human life which cannot be construed as being "religious," since all that transcends man's biological nature is perceived as being within the realm of religion. Robertson points out the need for a master conception of religiosity

> which will at one and the same time transcend the religious definitions of particular religious groups and also not be too general as to make redundant such questions as: Is society x more religious than society y?[2]

Robertson also notes that one of the most frequent characterizations of religion and religious has been Paul Tillich's statement that religion has to do with that which concerns us ultimately.[3] It is further assumed, by many, that all societies have ultimate concerns. The functional approach to religion which defines it in terms of its concern with 'ultimate problems' has been frequently criticized for being arbitrary and capricious in deciding what is ultimate and what is not.

However, it can be said that there are some human problems that clearly raise the question of ultimacy. Death is one such problem; sudden tragedy is another. We are creatures of reflection and as such we are aware of the limits to our present existence. The process of decay and final termination is inescapable insofar as it happens all around us. The appropriate focus for the sociological researcher is to pose the possibility of ultimate problems to the respondent and then to chart his reaction. This clearly avoids the pitfall of letting the respondent define ultimacy, since this has been done by the researcher in selecting the kinds of problems. It is not required of the sociologist that he define the 'essence of religion.' What is required is that he listen to the responses from the data sources with an open mind and make his own biases clear before interpretating the data.

This volume is a report on a survey of the American adult population in which many different forms of 'religious' questions were asked. We have attempted to get beneath the surface of religious affiliation, devotion, and dogma, and to penetrate into the area of basic beliefs or ultimate values. Another way of expressing this is to say that we are concerned with exploring human cosmologies. The principal purpose of this exploration has been to develop and test a set of survey items which will reflect ultimate or basic values. To this end, we have added some questions which essay the responses of our population to fundamental life problems, such as death and tragedy, of the sort which all of us must face or at least contemplate facing during the course of our lives.

Recent efforts in the sociology of religion have pivoted around four research models: a secularization model, a social class model, a church-sect model, and the Protestant ethic model. Each of these has contributed to the understanding of religion in American society, and each has labored under serious handicaps and deficiencies.

*(1) The secularization model.* In this perpsective, the principal concern has been the alleged decline of religious belief and practice in the face of the pressures of modern scientific and seculary society (see for example, the work of Charles Y. Glock and his associates, especially Glock and Stark, *Religion and Society in Tension*).[4] Church attendance and agreement with basic doctrinal propositions (the inspiration of the Bible, belief in a "personal" God, for example) were measured, and either the younger generation was seen as more "secular" than the older, the better educated more "secular" than the less educated, or the whole population more "secular" than its ancestors were presumed to be, usually at some unspecified point in the past. "Secular" frequently meant that the respondents were more likely to say "agree somewhat" instead of "agree strongly" when compared with the responses of the particular control group.

This approach has been subject to severe criticism. It has been argued that equating religion with church attendance, doctrinal acceptance, and the other measures normally used in religious survey research is theoretically naïve. It has also been contended that there is little survey evidence from the past in which the "secularity" of previous generations can be compared with the "secularity" of the present generation. Finally, it has been suggested that even granting the sake of the argument or the point that the secularization researchers make, the valid conclusion to be drawn is not that religion is declining but rather that fundamentalist Christianity is declining; and given the phenomenal success of the fundamentalist churches in recent years (see Dean Kelly), even this point appears dubious.[5]

*(2) The social class model.* A second tradition, fancying itself influenced by Marx and to some extent Weber, has attempted to see religious behavior as a function of social class membership.

Religion, it is suggested, is a form of cultural behavior expected of the middle and upper-middle classes and is either similar to or the same thing as a wide variety of other organizational behaviors that are also expected of the same class (see, for example, Demerath, Goode, Estus and Overington, etc.).[6] An alternative version of this approach (found in the work of Glock) is to see religion as a response to "need deprivation"—those classes or groups (women, black, old, downwardly mobile) who are caught in some sort of disadvantageous social position are, it is said, the most likely to turn to religion for consolation and comfort in their deprivation.

Two major criticisms have been leveled at this research tradition. First of all, it has been argued that the notion of social class used is naive in the extreme and shows little awareness of the sophistication of the Marxist or Weberian definitions of class. Usually, in this research tradition, "class" is equivalent to education or occupation or income or some combination of the three; the self-consciousness that Marx or Weber would have required as part of the definition of a class has usually not been investigated. All that the researchers in this tradition have proven is that people with higher incomes are more likely to go to church.

But, according to the second criticism, this is not that much more likely. The "class" differences in religious behavior reported by this tradition rarely exceed seven or eight percentage points; "class," in other words, explains rather little of the variance in religious behavior in the American population. It may be a variable that has to be considered in any causal model explaining behavior, but it is not a critically important variable. In a survey of American Catholics, social class accounted for only six percent of the variance out of a total of sixty-three percent explained variance.[7]

*(3) The church sect model.* In this perspective, the organizational structure of American religious groupings is seen as a correlate, if not a cause, of religious behavior. (See, for example, the work of Eister and the church sect aspect of the Goode-Demerath dialogue.)[8] The large, formal church structures tend to lead to a religious observance that is formal and appropriate for an elaborate organizational bureaucracy which demands certain limited and specified commitments from its members. The small, enthusiastic religious groups, on the other hand, tend to require a much

more diffuse and total commitment from their members. The former, it has been suggested by some, is more likely to be found among the middle class while the latter might be more appropriate for those members of the lower class who, in fact, engage in religious behavior at all.

The principal theoretical weakness of the church-sect approach is that it has never been able to solve the definitional problem of what is a church and what is a sect. Even the enthusiastic fundamentalist groups within American society quickly develop a rather elaborate organizational structure; and the most formal of church organizations seem to have within them room for enthusiastic small groups. Thus, pentacostalism has swept both Anglican and Catholic denominations in recent years—and it is hard to be more of a "church" in American society than these two denominations. Enthusiasm does, indeed, lead to more total religious commitment, but this seems to be true almost by definition; and enthusiasm can occur in a large church while bureaucracy can very quickly rear its routinizing head even in a commune.

*(4) The Protestant ethic model.* The proponents of this tradition (most notably, Gerhard Lenski writing in *The Religious Factor*), using what some would call a vulgarized form of Weber's classic theory, have attempted to relate "need achievement" with Protestant church affiliation and use such an "ethic" to explain the greater economic achievement of Protestants in American society.[9] Unfortunately for this approach, almost all the recent empirical research shows that the "achievements" of Catholics in the United States are now equal to those of Protestants (and in the case of Irish Catholics, higher). Some of the diehard Protestant "ethic" researchers point out that this is merely proof that American society has succeeded in "Protestantizing" the Catholic immigrants. Such a response can be neither proved nor disproved, but a more likely explanation for the upward mobility of the children and grandchildren of the turn of the century immigrant groups is the economic prosperity of the last three decades and the availability of opportunity for higher education since World War II for large numbers of the Catholic population.[10] That the Catholic groups have become "acculturated" (more or less) to American society is doubtless the case, but "acculturation" means "Protestantization" only if one defines it so on a priori grounds.

It is surely true that religious belief and practice are different in urban industrial society than they were in a rural agricultural society. It is also true that there is a modest relationship between income and church affiliation. It is likely that some small religious group (whether in a "church" or in a "sect") is both the cause and the effect of religious enthusiasm; and it is finally doubtless the case that religious traditions are also the bearers of cultural norms, of which high need achievement may be one (and it is apparently even more strongly linked with the Jewish, Greek Orthodox, and Irish Catholic traditions than it is with the British Protestant). Hence, there have been useful contributions made to our understanding of religion by the research traditions described in the previous paragraphs.

The authors of this report, however, prefer to assume a different focus because of the definitional problems surrounding the concept of 'religion' within the discipline of sociology. Robertson argues for "conformity to the ordinary cultural connotations of 'religion,'" with which we would agree.[11] We would prefer to talk about the 'sociology of basic beliefs' or a 'sociology of ultimate values' because we are convinced that 'religion' is not limited to dogma, doctrine, devotion, or ritual, but rather is a set of cultural convictions concerning the individual's, or the society's, perception of transcendent reality. These convictions may become manifest in a body of doctrine, or in ritualistic practices, or even in ecclesiastical structures over a period of time, but it is not a corollary of their existence that they will. These 'basic beliefs' or 'ultimate values' are man's way of struggling with the ultimate questions of the meaning and purpose of life which are raised by the fact that man knows about and reflects on the inevitability of his own termination. The evidence of mortality is all around us, and we are driven to determine if transcendent reality is malicious, benign, or simply neutral.

This approach to studying 'religion' borrows heavily from the cultural anthropologists, particularly Clifford Geertz, and from those sociologists working in the area where the sociology of knowledge and the sociology of religion mingle, particularly Peter Berger and Thomas Luckmann.

Geertz observes that man is a creature suspended in webs of meaning that he himself has spun. The most pertinent of Geertz's

work for our present purposes are his *Islam Observed* and the recent collection of essays entitled *The Interpretation of Culture.*[12]
Unlike their fellows in the animal kingdom, human children are born with a rather undeveloped set of instincts. They are not, as it were, preprogrammed by an instinctual system to respond to the wide variety of stimuli that they encounter in daily life. They must, rather, learn to organize and interpret experience so that they may be able to respond to it. Just as most "templates" for behavior are inherited by other animals, so they must be learned by humans. It is necessary for humankind to put meaning into a situation before a response can occur. (Geertz has a marvelous introductory chapter in his selected essays about the various ways of interpreting the wink of an eye and the different sorts of responses which may follow from different interpretations.) Like it or not (and frequently we do not), we are necessarily and inevitably an interpreting, meaning-seeking animal.

These meaning systems, which are the templates and the patterns by which we shape our behavior, constitute the human culture that we acquire from our parents and surrounding society and which we, in turn, pass on, doubtless modified by our own and our contemporaries' experiences, to those that come after. Culture is made up of a variety of such meaning systems (or interpretative schemes, to use Luckmann's word) that are appropriate for the different situations in which humans find themselves.

Geertz's concept of culture is a semiotic one. That is, it is intended to interpret signs and to reveal meaning. Therefore, the process of investigating 'culture' is not one of discovering laws and principles, but rather one of searching for meaning. Geertz relates this search for meaning to the sociology of religion in the following way:

> It [tracing of the social and psychological role of religion] is a matter of understanding how it is that men's notions, however implicit, of the 'really real' and the dispositions these notions induce in them, color their sense of the reasonable, the practical, the humane, and the moral[13]

Other pertinent questions for the sociologist have to do with how deeply and how effectively this "coloration" takes place. A religion, according to Geertz, is the effect of the notion of the "really real" in people's lives and in their societies. He elaborates in the following working definition:

> A religion is: a system of symbols which acts to establish powerful, pervasive, and long-lasting moods and motivations in men by formulating conceptions of a general order of existence and clothing these conceptions with such an aura of factuality that the moods and motivations seem uniquely realistic.[14]

A religion, according to this definition, serves both as a "model for" and a "model of" reality. A "model of" reality presents relationships in such a way as to render them apprehensible. It expresses the structure of the realtionships in synoptic form. A "model for" reality is the reverse of the above; it creates relationships according to some previously attained apprehension of reality. An architectural structure and a set of blueprints can serve as an analogy for these two concepts. We might go through the structure and chart all the physical relationships we could find and produce a set of blueprints which would be a "model of" the structure. On the other hand, we might know what kind of building was needed and sit down to draw out all the physical relationships on paper; in which case the blueprints become a guide or a "model for" the final structure.

A religion, and especially the symbols associated with it, is "ultimate" in the sense that it provides both an interpretation, or a "model of," for dealing with the most complex human problems such as suffering, death, and the experience of limitation at many levels, as well as a conviction that reality is interpretable, or a "model for." This dual function gives religious symbols varying degrees of power in different societies and makes them complex objects of investigation.

Man is very vulnerable in this world. Many things can harm him and he is well aware of the fact that physical existence ends at some time in the future. Social injustices and evils of all kind abound, and the evidence would seem to indicate that there is nothing much in the way of a plan for humankind. However, Man is able to do more than react to a "model of" which is presented before him; he is able to create a "model for" from that which he observes. Religion, as Geertz notes, is the modest assumption that

God is not mad; or, to put it more prosaically, it is the modest—but very critical—assumption that existence is not pure chaos. Even to say that life is ultimately absurd is at least to develop a proposition that itself has meaning and according to which one can shape one's reactions to the most basic questions of life. If the universe is ultimately uninterpretable—even with the interpretation of despair—then the underpinnings of all other attempts at interpretation are removed and one is caught in cosmic chaos, a situation which is intolerable for virtually all human adults.

We can leave aside for the purposes of the present work whether there are humans who are able to live and work without essaying some tentative answers to the questions of good and evil, life and death, comedy and tragedy. It is surely the case that most people cannot, and it may well be the case, as Edward Shils, following Durkheim, has suggested, that no "serious" person can avoid asking ultimate questions.[15] But our purpose in this present work is not to ask whether every human has a religion in the Geertzian sense, but rather to determine what the religious interpretative scheme is of that overwhelming majority of Americans who do at least on occasion ask questions of ultimate meaning.

Like all notions that are of critical importance, humankind tends to express its religions in symbols, and not only or merely in prose propositions. Images, pictures, stories, and rituals are incarnated religious insights which purport to explain what ultimate life, reality, and the world are all about. In the present work, we have not been able to trace in any great detail the linkage between symbol and interpretation—though God is clearly the central, the "privileged" symbol (to use Paul Ricoeur's word) of most religious systems.[16] Tell me who your God is and I will know what you believe about life and death, cosmos and chaos, good and evil. Our limited purpose at the present time, however, is to sketch an overview of the prose statements of the basic beliefs (or ultimate values) of the American population. At a later date it may be possible to go more deeply into the question of the relationship between religious symbols and the insights they express and incarnate—though that would be stretching the wisdom and the techniques of survey research far beyond their present capacities.

The second tradition which has influenced our work is the study of the transmission of values and, in particular, the very limited work that has been done on the transmission of religious values. Caplowitz noted in the early 1960s that those who had left their childhood religion frequently came from families where there was a high level of tension either between the parents or between parent and child.[17] Kotre was able to explain much of the variance in religious self-definition of graduate students in terms of their childhood experiences in the family interaction network.[18] Greeley *(The Denominational Society)* notes similar phenomena.[19] Finally, McCready, in his research on religious socialization among American Catholics, was able to explain approximately sixty percent of the variance in Mass attendance, and lesser amounts in other behaviors and attitudes, with a socialization model.[20] Particularly important in the model was the religious behavior of the father, and, in the case of the male respondents, the quality of the relationship between mothers and fathers. Since he was dealing with three generations, McCready was able to replicate the findings of his first- and second-generation relationships with the relationships between the second and third generations. (In a later work, McCready and his wife suggested that basic world view was strongly related to sexual identity and that one's view of the nature of the cosmos and one's view of oneself as a male or female may well be acquired at the same time, if not by the same process.[21]

We do not yet have the resources to test this hypothesis, but in the present work we are able to ask (of our adult respondents) how the basic belief systems were influenced by their parents' behavior and how adults, in turn, transmit their basic beliefs to their adolescent children.

It should be emphasized that our efforts are exploratory. We are engaged in what we believe is a radically new approach to the study of religion. Most of our measures and techniques are being used for the first time. Our analytic techniques are new in religious research. Our theoretical assumptions are still rough and unrefined —as are all assumptions before they are tried in the crucible of data collection. As in all preliminary exercises, wise researchers hopes to profit from mistakes and are flattered if other researchers are able to go beyond what they have done.

A heroic act of faith was required to believe that the techniques of survey research could get at the fundamental and ultimate beliefs of a population sample. Survey research has many serious limitations—as, be it noted, do all other research techniques. The way questions are worded, the tone with which an interviewer asks a question, the mood of the respondent at the time of the interview, the capacity of a survey item to plumb the depths of a person's thoughts and feelings, the quality of analytic techniques used, the biases of the researchers themselves—all of these make survey research a useful, but scarcely perfect or infallible way of describing and analyzing reality.

On the other hand, the survey method does have the advantage of dealing systematically with a representative population sample. It may tell us less about an individual than a long, in-depth interview by a trained clinician would. But it does deal with representative respondents and can provide general pictures of what is going on in a large population, something which the in-depth interview cannot do, save at prohibitive costs. Furthermore, good survey researchers (like all good researchers) are aware of the limitations of their method, are restrained in their interpretations, and continuously try to improve their techniques. From one point of view, the present effort is an attempt to develop a technique for exploring an area for which hitherto survey research has not developed appropriate techniques. We would not contend that our approach is the only valid way to study basic belief systems, but we do believe that it is one way to do such a study—a way which, in conjunction with other research techniques, holds promise of deepening our knowledge of how humankind wrestles with ultimate questions.

In the course of designing our survey instruments, we decided to use three techniques to measure the basic beliefs of the American population. The most innovative (and one suggested by Professor Geertz) was a series of vignettes asking respondents how they would respond to a critical life situation (and our interviewers reported excellent cooperation with those questions, which seemed to fascinate respondents and, in some cases, even move them to tears as they thought of how they did respond to a terminal illness in the family). We also used as a backup system a rather lengthy series of more traditional survey "agree-disagree" items. Finally, as the last, "fail safe" method, we asked a number of quite simple questions about the respondent's confidence in the survival of the human personality after death, the goodness of life, and the actuality of God.

Most of the present report will lean heavily on a rough and ready religious typology derived from the responses to the vignette items. We find those items to have been the most interesting and were frankly delighted to see that they worked so well. However, in Chapter 5, we will show the relationship between this belief typology and the other measures of basic belief which we attempted.

We have not been interested primarily in the change in ultimate values in American society because no measures like our own were attempted in the past. We do not know what proportion of the American population were "pessimists" in bygone years. Hopefully, our measures can be repeated periodically in years to come so that changes in the distribution of the American population on our belief typology, or more sophisticated ones that may be developed, can be measured.

We must note, however, that the increased proportion of pessimists in the younger age groups is not a particularly benign omen for our society. Strictly speaking, it is impossible to say on the basis of a one-shot survey whether this phenomenon is life cycle (characteristic of young people at whatever time), generational (characteristics of this particular generation because of its own unique experiences), or secular (a long-term trend). Our own hunch, based on our theoretical assumption that the broad outlines of a basic belief system are acquired in childhood and adolescence, is that the phenomenon of an increase in pessimists is probably more generational than cyclical. There is also some sign among our adolescent respondents that it may not be a secular trend. Obviously, more research is required on this presumably critical religious and social problem.

In the next chapter, we will describe in detail the life crisis vignettes that were used, the analysis which established that the theoretically expected response patterns did indeed emerge, and the ultimate value typology which was constructed from the vignette responses. In the third chapter, we will analyze the demographic composition of the value types; in the fourth, we will turn to the family social structures from which the various types come;

in the fifth, we will consider the relationship of ultimate values to more traditional religious measures; in the sixth, we will see if the quality of life is affected by ultimate values; and in the seventh, we will see if there is any relationship between these values and more proximate social attitudes. Chapter 8 will be concerned with paranormal experiences, and Chapter 9 will examine the influence of parochial education on ultimate values. In Chapter 10, we will deal with the adolescent children of our respondents. Finally, in Chapter 11, we will summarize and conclude this preliminary report with a description of plans for further analysis, as well as the further research that seems to be indicated.

We have been especially interested in paranormal experiences and, in particular, experiences of mystical ecstasy (see Chapter 8). This interest is partly curiosity, but there are solid theoretical and methodological justifications for the emphasis. It seems at least probable that most basic belief symbols are the result of individual or collective religious experiences (humankind may not so much create God in its own image and likeness as it may create itself in the image and likeness of the ultimate it experiences in moments of peak insight or ecstasy). Furthermore, a measure of basic belief that does not relate rather strongly to such experiences could seem to be of questionable value for religious researchers. Hence, a correlation between ecstasy (at least frequent ecstasy) and basic belief acts as a rough validation check on our measures.

We should perhaps note that ours is an exercise in the analysis of culture—in the sense of Weber and Geertz—i.e., that culture is the activity by which humans impose meaning on their experience. We are not engaged in a social-psychological enterprise. The vignettes used in our survey instrument were not intended to be projective tests designed to probe beneath the consciousness of our respondents. Obviously, there are close links between culture and personality, between identity and ideology, to use Erikson's terms. The psychological experiences of childhood and youth surely have an effect on the development of a system of ultimate values. These values, in turn, affect the psychological style and color of adult behavior. But our primary concern is with culture, not personality, with ascribed meaning and not the subconscious and unconscious motivations which might be related to the imposition of meaning on a given social situation. The present report is preliminary not merely in the sense that our research is a preliminary reconnaissance into uncharted areas, but also in the sense that the report is merely the first and introductory analysis of the data which we have collected.

We will sketch out in these pages the broad outlines of our findings. More detailed analysis, both scholarly and popular, will be undertaken in subsequent books, articles, and papers. It is to be noted that we are ready to share our data with any interested researcher.

# NOTES

1. Roland Robertson, "Religious and Social Factors in the Analysis of Secularization," in *Changing Perspectives in the Scientific Study of Religion,* ed. A. W. Eister, New York: Wiley, 1974, p. 57.

2. Roland Robertson, *The Sociological Interpretation of Religion,* New York: Schocken, 1970, p. 28.

3. Ibid., p. 24.

4. Charles Y. Glock and Rodney Stark, *Religion and Society in Tension,* Chicago: Rand McNally, 1965.

5. Dean Kelley, *National Catholic Reporter,* December 19, 1973.

6. *Journal for the Scientific Study of Religion,* Spring 1967.

7. William C. McCready, *Faith of Our Fathers: A Study of Religious Socialization,* Ph.D. dissertation, University of Illinois at Chicago, 1972 (university microfilms).

8. *Journal for the Scientific Study of Religion,* op. cit., p. 77.

9. Gerhard Lenski, *The Religious Factor,* Garden City, N.Y.: Doubleday, 1961.

10. Andrew M. Greeley, *The Denominational Society,* Glenview, Ill.: Scott, Foresman, 1972, p. 16.

11. Robertson, 1970, op. cit., p. 47.

12. Clifford Geertz, *Islam Observed,* New Haven: Yale Press, 1968, and *The Interpretation of Cultures,* New York: Basic, 1973.

13. Geertz, 1973, op. cit., p. 124.

14. Ibid., p. 90.

15. Edward Shils and Talcott Parsons, *Toward a General Theory of Action,* Cambridge: Harvard University Press, 1951.

16. Paul Ricoeur, *The Symbolism of Evil,* Boston: Beacon Press, 1967, pp. 232-278.

17. Greeley, op. cit., p. 242.

18. Ibid.

19. Ibid., p. 243.

20. McCready, op. cit., pp. 99-100.

21. William C. McCready and Nancy A. McCready, "Socialization and the Persistence of Religion," *Concilium,* Vol. 1, No. 9, 1973.

# Chapter 2

# A TYPOLOGY OF ULTIMATE VALUES

The primary benefit, for an individual, in having a set of values or beliefs which describe and proscribe ultimate reality is that he is saved from living with a pervasive and debilitating chaos. Unless we feel that we know how life works, or how it seems to work most of the time, we are plunged into chaotic uninterpretability in which the best we can hope for is day-to-day survival. People need more than short-term assurances. Unless we have the sense that existence is stable and usually sensible, we will be unable to cope with the tragedies and unexpected events which do happen from time to time. Another way of phrasing it would be to say that if everything that happened were random and unintelligible, how would we integrate those occurrences which truly seem to be random and unintelligible? If everyday life made no sense, then a tragedy, such as the death of a young person, would be shattering. Man clings to the interpretability of small, everyday things and builds a sensible universe from the accumulation of tiny understandings.

In earlier and simpler societies, the belief systems were most likely unitary ones, expressed by the legitimated cultural authorities of the tribe, the church, and the state. These societies were less pluralistic than ours and defined the essential terms and answered crucial questions for their members in such a say as to be acceptable to most of their people. The dissenting opinions were not given voice very often, and traditional authority was the common force behind the system of beliefs. Primitive people turned to shamans, witches, sorcerers, and others, who were reputed to know "what was really going on," in order to find the true explanations for everything from crop failures to death. The power of these people came not from their ruses or magic, but from their knowledge and wisdom. Men in earlier times, given relative differences in technological knowledge, were probably no more or less gullible than they are today. There is little reason to suspect that more primitive peoples were taken in by the trappings of their wise men anymore than modern peoples are. What they were looking for was knowledge about the unexplainable events in human life, and they honored, feared, and respected those who gave evidence of having such knowledge. Castenada makes this point dramatically in his discussion of the Yaqui sorcerer Don Juan.[1]

The most powerful stimulus for seeking to understand how reality is ordered emmanates from our reflection on our own deaths. What happens after death? This has been the central question for humankind since prehistory. We seem compelled to believe that *something* happens after death, although the descriptions offered are myriad. Perhaps primitive people really did think that death was the result of some inner creature deciding to leave the body. We moderns may scoff at their naivete, but in light of the evidence before them, theirs may have been the best possible answer. Contemporary medical science has succeeded in describing what happens organically during death, but the exact definition is still an open question.

As societies multipled and as science discovered more answers to the perplexing questions of life, belief systems became more differentiated. There arose many explanations and sets of guidelines for living. The templates for thinking about ultimate questions became diversified. However, the need to have a set of answers did not vanish with the arrival of rational scientism. The sticky questions of life and death remained, and they required answers, usually in symbolic form.

Symbols are of many different kinds. Some are very pragmatic and immanent, such as the octagonal stop sign, and others are abstract and transcendent, such as the Christian cross. Their origins are frequently shrouded in legend and myth, but the latter kind, the transcendent symbol, has a power which is often difficult to describe. Joseph Campbell offers this description in a discussion of the origins of what he calls 'creative mythology':

> Mythological symbols tough and exhilarate centers of life beyond the reach of vocabularies of reason and coercion. . . . The first function of a mythology is to reconcile waking consciousness to the 'mysterium tremendum et fascinans' of the universe *as it is:* the second being to render an interpretive total image of the same, as known to contemporary consciousness.[2]

The 'consciousness of the universe as it is' corresponds to man's most ultimate questions about the meaning of life. It is very difficult to have a set of words which suffices as a template, a shaper of ultimate meaning systems. Human beings are much more likely to create a set of images that represents ultimate reality in a clear and perduring manner.

These images form a 'mythos,' a representation of the way things really are, which can be passed along from generation to generation and which serves to make unexpected events interpretable. These modern 'mythologies' can also be considered as systems of basic beliefs or ultimate values which shape our understanding of events and circumstances.

In our pluralistic society, it is unreasonable and impractical to search for one set of symbols that represents a single system of belief. There are many different traditions from many diverse places represented in our society. Each of them has developed and communicated its own particular set of answers to the ultimate questions of life. Children absorbed these ultimate values and beliefs during their socialization experience, and they in turn modified them and passed them along to their own children. As generation upon generation went through this process, many different systems of interpretation and many different templates for reality were created. It was necessary, for the purposes of defining a research project, to narrow the range of systems down to a manageable size. We could not hypothesize an infinite variety of individual belief systems, for that did not correspond to the few science has uncovered relating to human behavior. People tend to group into homogeneous subpopulations along almost any variable one can imagine. It made sense to hypothesize that ultimate beliefs would be no different and that the society would be split into some manageable number of basic meaning systems, each of which would represent a particular orientation toward ultimate reality.

Having decided to attempt to measure basic meaning systems, we were faced with the problem of what the likely sets of interpretation might be in American society. Since no one had approached this question before, there was no literature to fall back on for guidance. What was the possible range of responses to ultimate issues available to humankind in contemporary America—or, indeed, to humankind at any time in its history?

We finally decided to take our cue from Paul Ricoeur's classic mixture of anthropology, archaeology, comparative religion, and philosophy, *The Symbolism of Evil.*[3] According to Ricoeur, there have been four fundamental responses to ultimate questions of good and evil—the optimistic (which Ricoeur sees in Egyptian religion); the pessimistic (as represented by Mesopotamian religious symbols); the fatalistic (to be found in post-Homeric Greece); and the hopeful (as manifest by the Israelites' religion).

The optimistic world view sees reality as ultimately good, though tinged with some sadness and evil which are not of major moment. The pessimistic sees the world as a cruel, hostile, and unsympathetic place. The fatalistic perspective shares the same grim view, but, unlike the pessimistic, sees little point in attempting to deal with or manipulate the hostile powers which dominate the cosmos. Finally, the hopeful perspective does not deny the cosmic battle between good and evil, nor the apparent success of evil in the battle, but believes in the precarious triumph of good; in this perspective, death, evil, and suffering have much to say., but they do not completely possess the last word.

It is obviously a long way from Ricoeur's typology to a survey questionnaire, but we responded that there might be six major ultimate value responses among modern Americans. The optimistic thrust, we speculated, might be divided into an uncomplicated religious optimism and an equally uncomplicated nonreligious or secular optimism. (We do not use uncomplicated in a pejorative sense, but rather to indicate that the belief system tends to minimize the problem of evil.) The pessimistic approach might be either fatalistic and resigned (like the Stoics) or angry. Between optimism and pessimism, we hypothesized a neutral stance in which the person expressed gratitude for past benefits. The hopeful approach, much as in the past, would tip the scales ever so slightly to favor of good in the cosmic war in heaven. Thus, the six possible interpretative responses to life problems would look something like this:

(1) Religious optimisms: "God will take care of everything, so there is no need to worry."

(2) Secular optimism: "Everything will turn out for the best somehow."

(3) Grateful acceptance: "We must be thankful for the good things that have happened to us despite the bad that we have to endure."

(4) Anger: "It is unfair and unjust that we should have to suffer."

(5) Resignation: "There is nothing that can be done; what will be will be."

(6) Hopefulness: "There is no denying the evil of what is happening, but the last word has not been said yet."[4]

Having arrived at these possible responses, we then began to think of ways in which we could measure the frequency of each of them in the population.

We reasoned that these responses flowing from the ultimate value system of individuals would be observed only in real-life situations. Only when people could not use the routine interpretative schema of everyday life would they call upon this deep reserve of understanding. Therefore, we had to devise a way in which people during an interview situation, could assess their own interpretative schema. As with many research efforts, it is difficult to recall the first time the concept of presenting the respondents with "vignettes" came to light. There have been so many ideas from so many people that the initial occurrences of some of them seem shrouded in the past. One experience that certainly crystallized a lot of thinking occurred during a seminar at the Center for the Study of American Pluralism at National Opinion Research

Center in the spring of 1973. Clifford Geertz was our guest that day, and we were discussing the research problems involved in getting beneath the superficial concerns of the respondents and tapping their cultural values. Professor Geertz recommended that we ask people about tragedy and ecstasy in their lives. He felt it was particularly at these times, when the person was rocked by an unexpected event, that the ultimate values were most evident.

The culmination of this line of reasoning was to present the respondent with a series of situations depicting unexpected events and asking them how they would react. These came to be called the "vignettes."

## Description of the Vignette Items

These vignettes represent situations in which people find themselves from time to time. They are serious, unexpected events that require some interpretation. The individual must make some sense out of what has happened or else be faced with the possibility that life itself is meaningless. For those who never actually experience situations such as these, they represent the material upon which nightmares are based. The death of a loved one or some disaster which befalls a child are events which threaten to convert life into chaos. Two of the vignettes pose situations involving children, two of them pose the question of the meaning of death, and one of them presents the kind of natural disaster about which we read in the newspapers.

The first vignette asks the respondent to imagine that he has just found out that he is going to die in the near future. Many people have had the experience of intending to go to a doctor for a checkup only to find that they procrastinate about making the appointment. When they finally do make the appointment, they find that they harbor secret fears that the doctor will tell them they have a terminal illness and only a short time to live.[5] The manner in which a person reflects upon this situation should reveal whether his vision of ultimate reality is optimistic, resigned, angry, thankful, or hopeful. The exact wording of the first vignette, together with the percentage of the sample responding to each answer, is presented below.

## "Terminal Illness" Vignette

You have just visited your doctor and he has told you that you have less than a year to live. He has also told you that your disease is incurable. Which of the following statements comes closest to expressing your reaction?

*Percentage*

a. It will work out for the best somehow. . . . . . . . . . . . .     15

b. No one should question the goodness of God's decision about death . . . . . . . . . . . . . . . . . . . . . . . . . . . . . . .     17

c. There is nothing I can do about it so I will continue as before. . . . . . . . . . . . . . . . . . . . . . . . . . . . . . . . . . .     35

d. I am angry and bitter at this twist of fate . . . . . . . . . . .     5

e. I have had a full life and am thankful for that . . . . . . . .     21

f. Death is painful, but it is not the end of me . . . . . . . . .     6

I cannot answer this question. . . . . . . . . . . . . . . . . . . }

None of the above . . . . . . . . . . . . . . . . . . . . . . . . . }     15

Slightly more than one-third of the respondents chose the "resigned" response, while another fifth of them chose the "accepting gratitude" response (e). Another third of the sample chose one of the "optimistic" responses, either religious (b) or secular (a). Six percent of the respondents chose the "hopeful" response and five percent chose the "angry" response. Most people, fifty-nine percent, expressed a positive reaction of some kind. The majority of those remaining chose the "resigned" response, which may indicate they were overwhelmed with the feeling of helplessness that would naturally be a part of such a situation. Very few respondents expressed anger or bitterness. People may be more prepared for death than has been commonly thought.

The second vignette presents the situation of having a son drafted into a combat area. This was a very pertinent problem at the time the survey was in the field, since the Vietnam war was not over and the draft had not been ended. Given the frequency of conflict during this century, there are not very many people to whom this situation would be unreal. People fear that some unknown harm will befall their children even when the possibility of such harm is remote. The responses to this item reveal the individual's perception of ultimate reality as it affects those closest to him.

### "Draft" Vignette

Your son is very likely to be drafted and will be going into a dangerous combat area soon. Which of the following statements reflects your reactions?

|  |  | *Percentage* |
|---|---|---|
| a. | Somehow it will all work out | 18 |
| b. | If God wants it to happen it must be all right | 20 |
| c. | This happens to lots of people; you learn to accept it | 28 |
| d. | The lottery system is unjust since it does not take individual situations into consideration | 3 |
| e. | He has been a good son and we are thankful for that | 8 |
| f. | It is terrible, but God may provide some opportunity for him to grow and expand his life | 23 |
|  | I cannot answer this question. | 20 |
|  | None of the above | |

Approximately one-fifth of the sample chose the religious version of the optimistic response (b), while another fifth chose the secular version (a). Roughly the same proportion chose the hopeful response (f), while slightly more than one-quarter of the respondents chose the response we have labelled "resignation." The "grateful" response and the answer indicating anger garnered ten percent together. Over two-thirds of the sample, sixty-nine percent, chose some positive response to this situation. The most common response was resignation, which indicates that people perceive this as a situation that happens more or less randomly, and therefore there is no sense in getting too upset about it. If it were perceived as a very unjust occurrence, there would be a larger angry response. The danger in the situation is not critically important, and the large "hopeful" response indicates that few people expect their son to die in combat.

The third vignette presents the situation in which one of the respondents' parents is dying a death filled with suffering. The mystery of suffering is one of the most difficult for Man to understand because it seems to refute the possibility of a benevolent ultimate reality.

## "Parent's Death" Vignette

Imagine that one of your parents is dying a slow and painful death and try to figure out for yourself if there is anything that will enable you to understand the meaning of such a tragedy. Which, if any, of the following statements best expresses your state of mind in this situation?

*Percentage*

a. He/she is in pain now, but he/she will be peaceful soon . . . . . . . . . . . . . . . . . . . . . . . . . . . . . . . . . .  20

b. Everything that happens is God's will and cannot be bad. . . . . . . . . . . . . . . . . . . . . . . . . . . . . . . . . . . .  23

c. There is nothing to do but wait for the end . . . . . . . .  6

d. This waiting is inhuman for him/her; I hope it ends soon . . . . . . . . . . . . . . . . . . . . . . . . . . . . . . . . . .  14

e. We can at least be thankful for the good life we have had together. . . . . . . . . . . . . . . . . . . . . . . . . . . . . . . .  23

f. This is a tragedy, but death is not the ultimate end for us. . . . . . . . . . . . . . . . . . . . . . . . . . . . . . . . . . . . .  15

I cannot answer this question. . . . . . . . . . . . . . . . . . }
None of the above . . . . . . . . . . . . . . . . . . . . . . . . . }  10

The two most common responses were religious optimism (b) and gratitude (e); these were each chosen by twenty-three percent of the sample. Another twenty percent chose the "secular optimism" response (a). Fifteen percent expressed hopefulness (f), and fourteen percent were angry (d). In contrast to the previous vignettes, the resignation response was a very small six percent. The respondents could be very resigned about their own death, but not about the death and suffering of their parents. It seems that it is very difficult for one to apply one's meaning system to one's own situation, and not nearly as difficult to apply it to another's situation.

The fourth vignette poses the situation in which a mentally retarded child is born, and respondents are asked to react by selecting a response that approximates how they think they would feel. This is a situation that some parents go through and most parents fear at one time or another.

## "Retarded Child" Vignette

Imagine that you have just had a child and that the doctor has informed you that it will be mentally retarded. Which of the following responses comes closest to your own feelings about this situation?

*Percentage*

a. We will try to take care of this child, but it may have to be in an institution; either way it will all work out . . . . .          19

b. God had His own reasons for sending this child to us . . .          22

c. We must learn to accept this situation . . . . . . . . . . . .          29

d. I love the baby, but why me?. . . . . . . . . . . . . . . . . .          4

e. I'm just plain glad to have the child here . . . . . . . . . .          4

f. God has sent us a heavy cross to bear and a special child to love. . . . . . . . . . . . . . . . . . . . . . . . . . . . . . . .          23

I cannot answer this question. . . . . . . . . . . . . . . . . . ⎫
                                                                  ⎬    12
None of the above. . . . . . . . . . . . . . . . . . . . . . . . ⎭

Twenty-nine percent of the sample chose the "resigned" response, indicating that since there was nothing they could do about the situation they might as well learn to accept it. Approximately one-fifth of the respondents chose secular optimism (a), religious optimism (b), and hopefulness (f) each. The angry and grateful responses garnered less than ten percent together. People are more likely to express hopefulness when dealing with situations that involve children. The "hopeful" response to the vignette about having a son drafted was also chosen by twenty-three percent of the sample. Children trigger a recognition of the future, and this makes thoughts of continuation more reasonable.

The last vignette asks the respondents to think about hurricanes as an example of the natural disasters which plague humankind, and to try to make some kind of sense out of such occurrences. These reactions indicate the respondent's interpretation of the capricious nature of ultimate reality. What is the purpose of such events, if any? Twenty-eight percent of the sample chose the "hopeful" response to this vignette, and slightly fewer, twenty-seven percent, chose the "resigned" stance. One-quarter of the respondents chose the "religious optimism" answer (b). The remaining fifth was split among secular optimism, anger, and gratefulness. This vignette received the most "hopeful" responses of any of the six, which indicates that it is easier to be hopeful about something that does not have the permanence of death, but rather passes in time.

## "Natural Disaster" Vignette

Almost every year hurricanes level homes, flood towns, destroy property, and take human lives. How can we make any sense out of such disasters which happen, apparently, by chance? Which of the following statements best describes your answer?

|  | *Percentage* |
|---|---|
| a. We can never really understand these things, but they usually have some unexpected good effect . . . . . . . . . | 6 |
| b. We cannot know the reasons, but God knows them . . . . | 25 |
| c. We cannot know why these occur and we have to learn to live with that fact . . . . . . . . . . . . . . . . . . . . . . . | 27 |
| d. The government is responsible for seeing these disasters do as little harm as possible. . . . . . . . . . . . . . . . . . | 3 |
| e. I am grateful that I don't live in a hurrican area. . . . . . . | 11 |
| f. I am not able to explain why these things happen, but I still believe in God's love. . . . . . . . . . . . . . . . . . . . . | 28 |
| I cannot answer this question. . . . . . . . . . . . . . . . . . . ⎱ | |
| None of the above. . . . . . . . . . . . . . . . . . . . . . . . . ⎰ | 10 |

By using these vignettes, we have attempted to observe the respondent's cosmology at work.[6] Ultimate values are those which order the relationships among People, God, and Nature, and make it possible for individuals to understand the meaning of what happens to them. The question now before us is how to ascertain the underlying patterns, if any exist, in these data. The percentages reported in the description of the items are sufficiently divergent to indicate that people were not all lumping on one response. There is a range of responses for each of the items. For example, if there were one belief pattern being measured, there would have been a tendency for the responses to regularly single out the same categories in each of the vignettes.

Among those not familiar with survey work, there is considerable sympathy for the open-ended question. It is suspected that the researchers are trying to force reality into their own preconceptions. If the researchers are fools or incompetent or do not seek criticism from their colleagues, such may well be the case. However, the same researchers who will make up the precoded questions will also make up the coding categories for open-ended questions. If one expects to do any statistical tabulations, there is no way to get away from some reliance on the researcher's skills and objectivity. The goal of any survey innovation is a series of precoded questions that can be used by other researchers; the only question is how soon in the process one begins using precoded categories. It was our judgment after the pretest that we were ready to use precoded items.[7] Such judgments reveal how much of any research project is more art than science, more intuition than demonstrable reasoning. Whether these intuitive steps are justified or not can be estimated by how well the results 'work'; that is, how well they describe reality and whether or not interpretable findings emerge.

## A Typology of Ultimate Values

Like other decisions we were forced to make in this preliminary investigation, the assignment of responses to typological categories was somewhat intuitive and arbitrary, as preliminary work must be. The details of the formation of this typology are fully exponded in Appendix B, but, simply put, the process was as follows. First, we collapsed the six possible response categories for each of the vignettes into four: "secular optimism" and "grateful acceptance" became one; "anger" and "resignation" became a second; "religious optimism" was left as a third category; and "hopefulness" was left as a fourth category (a detailed description of these response labels was given above). We then combined these four categories by cross-tabulation into five types of ultimate values: pessimism, secular optimism, religious optimism, hopefulness, and diffusion. These are very much like the responses outlined previously, with the exception that "anger" and "resignation" have become pessimism, and "grateful acceptance" has been put with secular optimism.

Others might create different typologies, but in the absence of a more elaborate theory, other than the tenuous one we have derived from Ricoeur, the final test of our typology must be pragmatic: Does it relate to any major differences on other variables? This question will be addressed in the following chapters.

Table 2.1 presents an initial overview by summarizing the distribution of the American population among the five types of ultimate values. Approximately one-quarter are pessimists and one-fifth each are religious optimists and hopeful. Less than one-fifth each are secular optimists or diffused. Taken all together almost three-fifths of the sample expressed some type of positive world view.

We would expect to find these types distributed differently through different demographic groups of the population. The young and the minorities might be more pessimistic, as might the well-educated. Those from rural areas might well be more hopeful and optimistic since they have not experienced failures of urban society at close hand. Hope, which requires some commitment to an ultimate view of reality, would seem to be most invariant with demography and more evenly distributed throughout the population.

When considering the types as independent variables, we might well expect them to have some influence on the quality of the individual respondent's life. The positive and the hopeful should be happier people with more satisfying relationships. They should be more tolerant of people of other persuasions. They should express greater personal satisfaction with their state in life and, on the whole, contribute more to those around them.

The pessimists should be isolated from others and less than satisfied with their state of life. Their persuasion should also influ-

**Table 2.1: The Frequency Distribution of the Ultimate Value Types**

| Ultimate Value Type | Frequency | Percentage |
|---|---|---|
| Religious optimist | 320 | 22 |
| Hopeful | 326 | 22 |
| Secular optimist | 210 | 14 |
| Pessimist | 344 | 24 |
| Diffuse | 257 | 18 |
| Missing data | 10 | — |
| Total | 1,467 | 100 |

ence their children. A major question to be asked in this research is whether or not belief patterns are passed along from one generation to the next. Any examination of the quality of life in a society must include the question of transmission of values and perspectives. We hope to be able to discuss this question, with data from the children of our respondents, later in this report.

The quality of life and the way in which the members of a society define their own realities are so closely intertwined that they sometimes appear as one. We speak of a society expressing a mood or a tone. The stock market may react to a "collective mood" of the country without really knowing what that might be. As a substitute, those involved in the market project their own feelings and mood onto the people and institutions of the society.

The complexity of reality is such that direct causality between two variables is often impossible to establish. Why, then, do we talk in terms of 'connections' and 'mechanisms for influence'? There are three primary reasons. First, one is forced to think through the implications of one's causal assumptions, and therefore to be explicit about them. Second, a writer is able to organize and discuss the data instead of meandering around in uninterpretable correlation matrices. Third, it is only by specifying causal connections that one can return to them in later research and test them more thoroughly.

What we intend to do is to establish 'models' as tools for analyzing data; they are not intended as hard and fast descriptions of reality. The assumptions upon which these models are based are not arbitrary, but are based on what we think are solid logical, theoretical, and chronological reasons. The model is simply a tool for examining reality, and in some of the later chapters we will devise and describe several interesting models. In the next two chapters, we will present background information about the various groups in our ultimate value typology. First, we will present their demographic backgrounds and then the data on family structure and the religious behavior of the families in which they grew up.

# NOTES

1. Carlos Castenada, *The Teachings of Don Juan,* New York: Simon & Schuster, 1970.

2. Joseph Campbell, *The Masks of God: Creative Mythology,* New York: Viking Press, 1968, p. 4.

3. Paul Ricoeur, *The Symbolism of Evil,* New York: Harper & Row, 1967.

4. It must be said by way of exposing our own values that this is the world view to which both authors are committed, with, of course, considerable hesitation, doubt, and uncertainty.

5. This may be a unique property of the Irish with whom we are all too familiar.

6. Mary Douglas, *Natural Symbols,* London: Barrie & Rockliffe, 1970.

7. In pretesting, we used both open-ended and precoded response categories. Most respondents were able to choose a precoded answer with little or no difficulty. Additionally, most of the open-ended responses were easily placed in a precoded category.

It was also the case that the open-ended versions, particularly of the death-related vignettes, triggered emotional difficulties for some respondents who had recently suffered a serious tragedy. Therefore we decided to use the precoded items since they seemed just as informative and since our interviewers, well trained though they might have been, were not professional counselors.

*Chapter 3*

# THE DEMOGRAPHY OF ULTIMATE VALUES

It is meaningless to discuss values of American society without referring to the pluralistic nature of our country. Diversity is one of our society's most salient characteristics. Our people come from many different cultural and racial backgrounds. Religious diversity, linguistic diversity, regional diversity—all of these influence the way in which people interpret the events that happen around them. A demographic analysis of the various types of ultimate value perspectives is a first step in understanding the ways in which these perspectives might influence peoples' lives. If salient demographic differences can be demonstrated between the various types, the analysis also serves to strengthen the idea that the types are reflective of real differences in world-view or meaning systems.

Recent articles by the authors of this report have delved into the persistence of ethnically related diversity in the society and have found that even in the third and fourth generations interpretable differences can be documented.[1] Patterns of relating one's parents found in ethnographic literature are also found in college graduates several generations later. The respondents are a long way from the source of the pattern, yet traces of the pattern remain. Professor Reed, in writing about the cultural identity of the Southerner, observes that region can also provide a context for interpreting reality with similar effects.[2] There are predictable differences as to how respondents from diverse backgrounds will understand and integrate external events.

Therefore, if ethnic, regional, and sexual groupings, along with others, are indicative of the different cultural contexts in which ultimate values develop, we ought to notice variations in the distribution of subgroups among the five ultimate types. One's "cultural baggage," brought with one from an earlier time and place, ought to influence whether one is a "religious optimist" or a "pessimist." The differences in child-rearing patterns in our society for boys and girls ought to influence whether men and women are distributed among the types in the same manner. Racial and religious identities may influence how one sees the world and what kinds of symbols one uses to understand and give meaning to the confounding events that swirl about us.

This chapter has two distinct purposes. The first is to test the utility of the typology by examining its relationship to various subgroup characteristics within the American population. If there are differences between the subgroups as to which types they inhabit, and if there are logical speculations that can be made to explain the differences, then we may be more confident that the types represent different ways of viewing reality which exist within the population. The second purpose is to present a profile of the types. For example, who are the religious optimists? Demographic statistics will present a picture of the respondents in each of the types which will be referred to during succeeding chapters.

The technique for presenting these profiles will be to estimate the extent to which various social categories or population subgroups, the well-educated or males or Catholics, for example, are overrepresented or underrepresented in each type. (For an example of the way in which this method is used to analyze data from another source, see Verba and Nie's *Participation in America*.[3]) This measure is a ratio of the proportion of a particular social category found in a belief type to the proportion of that category found in the American population as a whole. In other words, let us assume that respondents under the age of thirty formed twenty percent of the sample population. If we discovered that they were ten percent of the "religious optimists," we would conclude that they were underrepresented in that type by fifty percent. The extent of over- and underrepresentation is a function of both the number of percentage points and the size of the group in the sample.[4] A five percent difference can generate a large over- and underrepresentation if the subgroup is a small segment of the entire population, whereas the same difference will not generate much disproportion in a subgroup that is a large segment of the population.

## Sex, Race, and Age Profiles

Table 3.1 shows the proportion of men and women represented in each of the five types. Men are underrepresented among the hopeful, while they are overrepresented in the last three types—secular optimists, pessimists, and diffused. Women show the opposite pattern, since they are just about one-half the sample. One way of looking at this table is to note that women are more likely to be specifically "religious" in their world view than are men. To the extent that men express a positive world view, they express it in a secular fashion rather than a religious one. Men are more likely to be pessimists than are women, and neither is particularly likely to be in the diffused type.

Socialization is a very different process for boys and for girls in our society. Boys are taught that they must learn to take care of themselves so that they can one day lead their own family and provide for its needs. Girls are taught that they will be cared for if they find the right man, and their needs will be provided for in the future just as they have in the past. Many girls have been socialized into dependent roles in which they are taught to look to

**Table 3.1: Proportion Overrepresented or Underrepresented in Ultimate Value Types by Respondent's Sex**

| Ultimate Value Type | Male | Female |
|---|---|---|
| Religious optimist | 0 | 0 |
| Hopeful | −29 | 25 |
| Secular optimist | 12 | −10 |
| Pessimist | 17 | −15 |
| Diffuse | 5 | −3 |
| N = | (687) | (780) |

someone else, usually a man, for their source of self-esteem. This is consistent with the observation that females in the sample are overrepresented in the two belief types that explicitly refer to the existence of God. Whether the deity is perceived as a "father figure", or whether this expresses the dependence that faithful people have on their God is a question that would require more intensive social-psychological research.

The fact that males are overrepresented in the secular optimism category might be a function of having been socialized to depend on themselves rather than on others. It is more difficult for a man in our culture to say, "I can't do this alone, I need some help," than it is for a woman. The secular optimism response to the situations posed by the vignettes is one that says the respondent thinks things will work out, but there is no indication of why. There is no dependence on a specific external force that will enable things to work out for the best.

The overrepresentation of males in the pessimistic categories may be the result of their greater contact with the successes and failures connected with the system of competition that dominates our society. Men are more likely to have been taught to compete, while women have not. This produces an awareness of success and failure in men which may well lead to a pessimistic set of ultimate values. Men often express the attitude that women do not know what the real world is like. This is taken to mean that they do not know what the depths of failure and the heights of success can do to the perspective of the individual personality toward the nature of ultimate reality. Since it is ordained by the nature of the competitive system that there be more losers than winners, men would be more likely than women to feel pessimistic about ultimate endings. The implications of these data for theories of socialization are certainly provocative. It may be that sex-role modeling as described by Biller and others may be linked to the absorption of ultimate values as hypothesized by McCready and McCready.[5] Male role-models may communicate more than the definition of maleness to their offspring; they may pass along basic ultimate values that describe the way in which life will really unfold—that is, pessimistically. Female models may, on the other hand, pass along values that describe the hopeful and optimistic scenario. The fascinating question is what happens when both parents are optimists or hopeful as opposed to having both parents pessimists. This question will have to await a more detailed analysis.

The representational ratios for the belief types according to the respondent's racial identity are presented in Table 3.2. The white respondents are neither over- nor underrepresented very much in any of the belief types. This indicates that they are evenly distributed throughout the five types and that there is no relationship between being white and possessing a particular set of ultimate values. Being black, however, does make a difference as to which type the respondent is likely to inhabit. (These results must be interpreted with great caution due to the fact that a representational sample does not give a very reliable picture of a small population subgroup.) Black respondents are overrepresented by about one-half in the religious optimism type and they are underrepresented in every other category except diffuse. The overrepresentation of blacks in the religious optimism category may be related to the "aggressive meekness" described by Pettigrew as the operational style of American blacks for many generations.[6] This style of dealing with the dominant white society precluded bitterness and anger as visible components. The reasons are obvious. "Charley" has the votes and the guns and the money. Dick Gregory says to a predominantly white audience:

> You don't see any bitterness in me. It doesn't mean I'm Tomming either. Most misused word in America today. You smile, some people say you're Tomming; say 'thank you,' you're Tomming. Everybody, one time or another, is an Uncle Tom. A cop stops you for speeding and you try to talk him out of it. You let him say things to you in a tone and language you'd never let anyone ordinarily get away with. That's a form of Uncle Tomism and you're not doing anything more'n try to get out of that ticket.[7]

Table 3.2: Proportion Overrepresented or Underrepresented in Ultimate Value Types by Respondent's Race

| Ultimate Value Type | White | Black |
|---|---|---|
| Religious optimist | −8 | 45 |
| Hopeful | 0 | −7 |
| Secular optimist | 3 | −15 |
| Pessimist | 6 | −36 |
| Diffuse | −1 | 12 |
| N = | (1,234) | (177) |

The historical "other-world" nature of black American religion provided an "aggressively meek" condemnation of the dominant white religions which said this was the best of all possible societies.[8] Black religion was more than escapism; it was a counter-religion which sought to correct and compensate for the misinformation and oppressive myth-building of the white-dominated religions in the society. As a result, it would be quite possible for many blacks to develop a basic belief that was in the category of religious optimism. It is important to note, however, that black religious optimism is probably not the same as white religious optimism.

Table 3.3 presents the representation ratios for the belief types according to the age of the respondents. Teenagers are most overrepresented in the diffused category, while being most underrepresented in secular optimism. Those in their twenties are most overrepresented in the pessimism type. Those in their thirties are still overrepresented among the pessimists. but tend to be more equally distributed throughout the rest of the types. The forties are the most hopeful and after that the respondents begin to be overrepresented in the religious optimism category and underrepresented in the pessimism category. Hopefulness tends to peak at forty and decline with age, and by the time the respondents in their seventies are observed, they are overrepresented in the secular and religious optimism category and underrepresented in the hopeful category.

The essential question when dealing with age categories is whether the impact of age on the data results from life-cycle dif-

Table 3.3: Proportion Overrepresented or Underrepresented in Ultimate Value Types by Respondent's Age

| Ultimate Value Type | AGE | | | | | | |
|---|---|---|---|---|---|---|---|
| | Less than 19 | 20-29 | 30-39 | 40-49 | 50-59 | 60-69 | Over 70 |
| Religious optimist | 18 | −29 | −20 | −10 | 20 | 50 | 26 |
| Hopeful | 16 | 2 | 0 | 41 | −8 | −34 | −33 |
| Secular optimist | −86 | −26 | 7 | −14 | 22 | 48 | 22 |
| Pessimist | −7 | 31 | 12 | −14 | −34 | −24 | 14 |
| Diffuse | 36 | 12 | 3 | −8 | 12 | −26 | −28 |
| N = | (55) | (361) | (261) | (249) | (241) | (170) | (127) |

ferences or from generational differences. Certain kinds of phenomena are the property of certain times of an individual's life. Death is more a concern of the old than of the young. Concern for the survival of one's children is more common when families are young rather than when they are old. Other phenomena are the property of generational experiences that are common to a large group of people. The Great Depression, for example, or World War II are indelibly imprinted on the personalities and the psychosocial structures of those who lived through the events. Experiences such as these differentiate between those who were growing to adulthood during those times and those who were too young to remember the events or who were not even born at the time.

There is no adequate way in which we can sort out generational and life-cycle differences in a one-time sample. (This is an important reason for viewing this project as a "bench mark" survey against which future surveys can be compared.) These data can be viewed as having either a generational or a life-cycle effect. The teenagers and middle-aged are most likely to be hopeful, while those in their twenties and thirties and the very old are most pessimistic. This may be due to something inherent in being a certain age or it may be due to the experiences people have had.

We can speculate that those in their twenties have lived through a time that has seen great social conflicts in and out of our country. They have seen three extremely charismatic leaders wasted becore their eyes. It may well be that pessimism about the nature of ultimate reality is an appropriate and understandable stance for them to take. On the other hand, those in their forties are at the peak of their powers, and many of them are achieving their life-long goals. This would tend to account for their hopeful perception of life. The society seems to be working as well as one could reasonably expect and they are likely to be confident of a benign future.

It is worth noting that the older respondents are less likely than usual to be diffuse and the teenagers are most likely to fall in this type. This also makes intuitive sense since teenagers are most likely to be unsettled in their ultimate values, while older people are much more likely to have become accustomed to thinking of the world in the same way for many years. As one approaches seventy or so and death becomes an inevitable concern, religious and secular optimism decline and pessimism increases. Hopefulness has started to decrease even earlier, and the picture resembles one of declining strength as people come to realize that we must all deal with the same unknown quantity at the end of life.

Another possible relationship between generational effect and life-cycle effect is that the two reinforce each other. The young may have certain tendencies toward pessimism which are derived from the insecurity produced by the events that a specific generation experienced. At the same time, the old have toward religious optimism—until death comes too close—certain tendencies which have been reinforced by the early experiences of a society in which everything worked as it should and there was unlimited possibility for expansion. Without successive studies at different points in time, these speculations can never be satisfactorily resolved. Possessing such information would make it possible to perform cohort and change analysis, but, deprived of time studies, all we can do is to speculate on the meaning of some of these differences.

## SOCIAL CLASS PROFILE

The relationship between the ultimate values typology and family income level, as shown in Table 3.4, is quite revealing. The optimists, both religious and secular, are well below the median income level for the population, while the diffuse are well above the median. The pessimists and the hopeful are both above the median, with the hopeful being twice as far from it as the pessimistic. Those of lower social position, as measured by income, are most likely to be optimistic, while those in more favorable circumstances are divided among the three remaining types.

Table 3.4: Respondent's Family Income by Ultimate Value Types

| Ultimate Value Type | Median Income (Dollars) | Difference from the Median |
|---|---|---|
| Religious optimist | $ 6,110 | −$3,490 |
| Hopeful | $10,475 | +$  875 |
| Secular optimist | $ 5,155 | −$4,445 |
| Pessimist | $10,039 | +$  439 |
| Diffuse | $11,442 | +$1,842 |
| Median | $ 9,600 | |

Table 3.5: Over- and Underrepresentation of the Ultimate Value Types in
Educational Categories

| Ultimate Value Type | Less than High School Grad | High School Grad | At Least Some College |
|---|---|---|---|
| Religious optimist | 59 | −17 | −100 |
| Hopeful | −24 | 17 | 12 |
| Secular optimist | 4 | −9 | 4 |
| Pessimist | −20 | −3 | 23 |
| Diffuse | −26 | 12 | 14 |
| Mean | 526 | 465 | 304 |

Since income alone does not measure one's position in our
society, we will also inspect the relationship between educational
attainment and the types of ultimate values.[9] We observe in Table
3.5 that there is not the consistency among the religious and
secular optimists that there was in Table 3.4. The only type which
is clearly not well educated is the religious optimist. The secular
optimists are just about even with their proportion in the population, and the hopeful, pessimistic, and diffused are all more
likely to be well educated.

These two tables indicate a strong negative relationship between
social status and religious optimism as a value system. The secular
optimists are more in the middle, having a strong negative relationship with income and almost no relationship with education.
Because of the intercorrelation of education and income, more
detailed analysis needs to be done on these relationships.

The religious optimists are neither well off economically nor are
they well educated. The secular optimists are poor, but they are
not substantially below the educational attainment one would
expect for them. The diffuse, the hopeful, and the pessimists all
tend to be well off and well educated, with the diffuse leading the
economic indicator and the pessimists leading in the educational
indicator. This latter fact could be taken as an indication of the
negative influence of higher education, in the sense that pessimism
is a negative state of mind. However, there is a confounding variable in that we also know that young people are more likely to be
well educated than older people. Which factor accounts for the
pessimism, being young, or being well educated?

We can conclude from Table 3.6 that age, and not education, is
the important variable in influencing pessimism. Note that for

Table 3.6: Percentage of Respondents in Ultimate Belief Types by Age and Educational Level

| Ultimate Value Type | High School or Less | | At Least Some College | |
|---|---|---|---|---|
| | Under 30 | Over 30 | Under 30 | Over 30 |
| Religious optimist | −4 | 32 | −59 | −41 |
| Hopeful | 9 | −5 | 0 | 23 |
| Secular optimist | −43 | 14 | −7 | 21 |
| Pessimist | 12 | −21 | 46 | 0 |
| Diffuse | 6 | −17 | 17 | 6 |
| N = | (236) | (755) | (224) | (240) |

Mean for Education = 15.1
Mean for Age = 33.3

both the college educated and the non-college educated, the older respondents are considerably less pessimistic. The well educated, over-thirty respondent is neither more nor less likely to be pessimistic than anybody else given the proportion of that group in the whole population. It should be further noted that a college education seems to attenuate the tendency to be a religious optimist rather drastically. Religious optimists are almost exclusively in the less well educated group over the age of thirty.

Age and education taken together do not have very much impact on hopefulness, although it is interesting to see that it is the college educated, older respondent who is more likely to be hopeful. This should be kept in mind as part of the reason for the separation of the two "religious" types, the religious optimist and the hopefuls. There are dramatic demographic differences between these two groups, yet on most surveys of religious attitudes they would tend to be lumped together in one, catchall category. Age also influences the secular optimist more than does education. These respondents are more likely to be older in both of the education classifications.

Although there is some indication that higher education influences students to be pessimistic, the stronger variable in all cases is age. This would lead us to conclude that one's ultimate value system is more influenced by life position than by immediate experiences. Education is one of the experiences of secondary socialization. Students come to school with all of the cultural and psychological baggage from their families, neighborhoods, and friendship groups. Where one is in the life cycle makes much more of a difference than what one is studying in terms of ultimate values. These value systems do appear to be different at different stages of life and therefore they are not set at birth to remain the same ever after. Adjustments are made by the individual, but they are less in response to immediate stimuli, such as education, and more in response to long-range stimuli, such as aging.

We see in Table 3.7 that the representational ratios for the categories of marital status within the types also reveal a life-position character. Those respondents who were married at the time of the survey were evenly distributed across the five types. Single people who had never been married were overrepresented in the pessimism categories by a large margin, and they were almost as highly underrepresented in one of the optimism categories, religious optimism. This is congruent with Bradburn's work on the correlates of happiness or psychological well-being.[10] Single people reported that they were less happy and satisfied with their lives than married people, and this would seem to be consistent with a finding of pessimism among the singles.

The last two categories of married status provide some interesting information about those who may be alone in society besides those who have not married. The divorced or separated are highly overrepresented in the pessimism category, while those who have been widowed are just as overrepresented in religious optimism. The widowed also tend to be overrepresented in the hopeful type. This indicates that separation from one's spouse by choice—that is, through a divorce or other legal proceedings—is more pessimism-producing than separation by the death of one's spouse. (It is worth noting that those who have been divorced or separated

Table 3.7: Proportion Overrepresented or Underrepresented in Ultimate Value Types by Marital Status

| Ultimate Value Type | Married Now | Single Never Married | Divorced or Separated | Widowed |
|---|---|---|---|---|
| Religious optimist | 0 | −29 | 0 | 42 |
| Hopeful | 5 | −4 | −20 | −26 |
| Secular optimist | 0 | −4 | −10 | 15 |
| Pessimist | −8 | 28 | 44 | 3 |
| Diffuse | 4 | 8 | −20 | −36 |
| N = | (1,074) | (173) | (95) | (115) |

Table 3.8: Proportion Overrepresented or Underrepresented in Ultimate Value Types by Ethnoreligious Groups

| | Protestant | | | | Catholic | | | | | Jewish | Black | No Religion |
|---|---|---|---|---|---|---|---|---|---|---|---|---|
| Ultimate Value Type | British | German | Scandi-navian | Irish | Irish | German | Italian | Polish | Spanish | | | |
| Religious optimist | −12 | −14 | 11 | 11 | −19 | 16 | −26 | 15 | 17 | −68 | 53 | −83 |
| Hopeful | 21 | 27 | 82 | 11 | 34 | −27 | −47 | 20 | 25 | −69 | −4 | −73 |
| Secular optimist | 39 | 23 | −55 | −32 | −26 | −43 | −45 | −15 | −14 | −28 | −7 | 9 |
| Pessimist | −18 | −27 | −49 | −23 | 19 | 14 | 65 | −12 | −26 | 77 | −38 | 121 |
| Diffuse | −16 | 2 | −1 | 28 | −23 | 26 | 32 | −12 | −4 | 75 | 1 | 12 |
| N = | (175) | (134) | (48) | (74) | (48) | (50) | (52) | (42) | (33) | (30) | (177) | (85) |

are overrepresented only in the pessimism type; they are propor-
tionate or underrepresented in all the rest.) One of the side effects
of a broken relationship is the loss of self-esteem and self-confi-
dence, coupled with a sense of failure. These emotions would be
closely linked with pessimism.

The loss of one's partner through death elicits a different world
view. The fact that the widowed are disproportionately found in
the religious and secular optimism types indicates that they may
be trying to "make the best of it." These two types reflect an
attitude that everything will somehow be fine in the future, and,
in fact, may be a way of glossing over the temporary but excruci-
ating sense of loss after the death of a partner. Once again we can
see that the ultimate values are related to life positions. It may be
useful for those people who work with the grieving to know that
relatively few of them are in the hopeful category. Further
research will be able to link ultimate values to stages of grieving
in a way that is impossible in this present effort, but the hopeful
stance would seem to be the most satisfactory set of values for
people experiencing this kind of loss. It does not present an easy,
shallow solution, but it does permit life to continue with purpose
and meaning rather than chaos and despair. If future research
could discover ways of guiding people toward hopefulness during
their times of crisis, much suffering and wasting of human re-
source could be avoided.

## ETHNO-RELIGIOUS AND REGIONAL PROFILE

We would expect that in a pluralistic society such as ours, there
would be interpretable differences between the different ethnoreligious subgroups, and the data, as presented in Table 3.8, bear
this out. There are clearly different patterns of ultimate values in
different groups. The Jews, the Italian Catholics, and those with
no religious affiliation are most underrepresented in the religious
optimism type and overrepresented among the pessimism and the
diffused types. The only respondents highly overrepresented in
the religious optimism type are the blacks in the sample. The
Scandinavians and the Irish Catholics are the most likely to be
hopeful, while the Jews and the Italians and those with no religion
are least likely to be in this category. The only people who are

overrepresented in the secular optimism type are the British and German Protestants. These data are interesting, but what is the best way to interpret them?

A technique used by the authors in other research has been to correlate descriptions from the country of origin to the data collected from the ethnic group in the country of migration. Most of these descriptions can be found in the ethnographic literature of anthropology and social history.[11] Congruence between the descriptions of the anthropologists and those provided by the analysis of these data is then taken to indicate the persistence of some portion of the "cultural baggage" of the immigrants over time. The essential research question is whether or not having any knowledge of the circumstances extant in the country of origin adds to our predictive powers concerning the ethnic group in this country. Previous research has answered this question affirmatively for some specific ethnic groups.[12] However, we do not possess the same quality information for all the groups in the society, so at best this is an exploratory technique.

The British Protestants were the first immigrants from Europe to come in large numbers, and they set the normative culture for those who followed. They are overrepresented in the hopeful and secular optimism types, which is consonant with a world view that says "anything is possible." The heritage of these immigrants was filled with the desire to escape an oppressive political and religious system and begin life anew in a free country.

The German Protestants have a typological profile quite similar to the British. They are more likely to be hopefuls and secular optimists than not, and they, too, were early immigrants. Theirs was a pragmatic and achievement-oriented heritage which, when transplanted, was likely to produce such a benign world view.

The Scandinavians are the group most likely to be hopeful. This does not exactly square with the stereotype of the sour and gloomy Scandinavian, but then some stereotypes are truer than others. One possible explanation is that these people are less likely to be in urban centers of population and are therefore less likely to be exposed to all the pessimism-producing stimuli of our large cities. Another possible explanation is that there is something in the heritage of the Scandinavian which is influential in producing people with a hopeful system of ultimate values. We do know that

Scandinavians have been increasing their proportion among those in our society who have risen the occupation-education ladder of prestige during recent years, and it may be that this success is associated with a hopeful outlook.[13] It is impossible to determine the causal direction in this relationship, of course, but the speculation is interesting.

The Irish Protestants are a most interesting group in our country. Most observers underestimate their number, probably because the Catholic portion of the Irish immigrants is so visible, but over half of those respondents choosing "Irish" as an ethnic background are Protestant. These people are overrepresented among the diffused type and less so among the religious optimists and the hopefuls. The Irish Protestants are a group who are not growing in status in the society, and there is some evidence that they are declining.[14] They are an invisible group to the rest of the society, and perhaps even to themselves in that they are not as likely as the Poles or the Italians, for example, to portray themselves as a distinct group with clear cultural traits and a national heritage. Diffusion represents their meaning system rather well, given our sketchy knowledge about their situation.

The opposite is true of the Irish Catholics. They are more likely to be both hopeful and pessimistic than we would expect given their proportion in the sample population. This is in accordance with our previous research findings that the Irish were likely to be high on measures of both trust and fatalism.[15] This group is the most successful of the immigrants, with the exception of the Jews.[16] Nevertheless, they face the world with a paradoxical view combining pessimism with hope, although it must be noted that the scales are tipped slightly in favor of hope.

The German Catholics, like the Irish Protestants, are most likely to fall in the diffused type. Although not as downwardly mobile as the Irish Protestants, this group is nowhere near as successful as the Irish Catholics.[17] Since there is no good hypothetical understanding of the diffused type, speculation as to what membership in it means is difficult; but it may be that this is what happens to people who are overshadowed or who lose sight of their heritage and replace it with nothing. German Catholics have been in this country for many years and have steadily lost control of the church to the Irish, while also watching the Irish move up the social system faster than they. A diffusion of the value system may well be associated with such a set of circumstances.

The Italians, on the other hand, are not only more likely to be in the diffused type, they are much more likely to be pessimists. There is no optimism in their typological profile at all, and they are underrepresented in all three of the benign categories. Writers have described the Italian family as an exclusive unit suspicious of outsiders and mistrustful of any authority save its own.[18] When the Italians immigrated to this country, many of their American-born offspring rejected traditional customs as part of the effort to become more like the American norm.[19] These influences, close family ties and the rejection of traditional ways, could work in tandem to produce a world view which is either diffuse or pessimistic. Either there is no meaningful set of ultimate values which is recognized by the individual, or the values which are recognized represent the frustration and sense of loss which accompanies the rejection of what was once a treasured heritage.

The Polish and Spanish Catholics are more likely to inhabit the hopeful or the religious optimism type than any other. It is interesting to note that their patterns look somewhat like that of the Scandinavians. Both these cultures have strong religious components, and in other data we have seen that the Poles have the strongest financial commitment to their church of any ethnic group.[20] Both these cultures seem to have a benign view of ultimate reality that transcends their immediate circumstances and needs and focuses on the ultimate graciousness or benevolence of God.

The Jews in the sample are most likely to be in either the pessimism or diffused type. The most salient characteristic about both these types is that they do not reference the supernatural at all. Judaism has reacted differently to secularization influences because it has a different starting point from most other religions in the United States.[21] The Jewish religion has an extremely wide notion of the sacred and sacramental perspective, as opposed to the moralistic perspective of most American religions. This means that there is a weak distinction between clergy and laity since both are always dealing with sacred things. American Jews have selected out those parts of the sacred system which they feel they can adhere to in this culture, and have dropped the remainder.[22] This division of their traditions has furthered the "this-world" focus of Jewish culture. There is not very much in the way of looking toward rewards stored up in heaven as there is looking at what one leaves behind on earth. This outlook would produce the kind of pessimism we have observed, and the fractionalization of the religious culture would produce diffusion.

Last, we will look at those who said that they had no religious affiliation whatsoever. It is interesting to note the difference between this group and the Jews. These respondents are most overrepresented in the pessimism type, rather than being split between pessimism and diffusion, as are the Jews. They have more of a pattern to their responses in the sense that they are most likely to see situations in a pessimistic light and most likely to reject either of the religious interpretations.

Our essential conclusion drawn from the data in Table 3.8 is that this typology of ultimate values is reflective of real and important differences within the population. It varies in accordance with the most deep-seated kinds of divisions in our pluralistic society in interpretable ways. Ethnic heritage is our best indicator of the "cultural baggage" brought to this country by the immigrants and the fact that this typology reflects heritage supports our contention that these vignettes are tapping into some basic cultural mechanisms of these respondents.

Another characteristic of our society, although it is often overlooked, is regional affiliation. Professor Reed, mentioned earlier, has written very persuasively that residence in the South sets one apart and provides an identity not unlike that of membership in an ethnic group.[23] Region may serve as a reference group for some people and not for others. State loyalties are said to be much stronger in the South than elsewhere, but we know very little about non-state-specific regional affiliation.[24] It may be that people of different regions have different world views due to many circumstances.

Some regions, such as the Northeast, are densely populated, which would tend to diminish optimism since residents are faced with the despair generated by our more complicated urban and bureaucratic problems on a much more intimate level. Other areas, like the South, have a character which is both unique and long-

Table 3.9: Proportion Overrepresented or Underrepresented in Ultimate
Value Types by Region

| Ultimate Value Type | Northeast | Midwest | South | West |
|---|---|---|---|---|
| Religious optimist | 0 | −14 | 32 | −18 |
| Hopeful | −29 | 3 | 16 | 12 |
| Secular optimist | −29 | 11 | −10 | 4 |
| Pessimist | 19 | −7 | −19 | 10 |
| Diffuse | 19 | 14 | −26 | −9 |
| N = | (339) | (418) | (335) | (365) |

standing. If there are differing perspectives in the different regions, they should be reflected in the typology of ultimate values.

The most striking feature of Table 3.9 is the overrepresentation of the South among the religious optimists, and the overrepresentation of the Northeast among the pessimistic and diffused types. The Midwest and the West do not show any clear patterns. (The assignment of states to regions is done according to standard Bureau of Census conventions.[25]) The fact that the South is so heavily represented in the religious optimism type is encouraging when we consider that this type is supposed to reflect a simple adherence to religious explanations and interpretations. The religious beliefs of an overwhelming proportion of Southerners focus on the literal and concrete interpretation of the Bible and on the fact that God is personally aware of what we do in our lives.[26] These people are hypothesized to be in the religious optimism category, and that is where the majority of them are.

The Northeast was also hypothesized to be in specific categories —namely, the Pessimistic and Diffused—and that is where they are most heavily concentrated. Taken together, these two facts are highly supportive of the validity of this typology. Whatever the reasons for regional differentiation—and they ought to be explored more fully—it coincides in an interpretable fashion with the typology of values.

RELIGIOUS PROFILE

A final characteristic which divides our population is religion. Just as the previous demographic traits have specified the typology, so does religious affiliation. Protestants are more likely to be either religious optimists or hopefuls, while Catholics are not

Table 3.10: Proportion Overrepresented or Underrepresented in Ultimate
Value Types by Religious Preference

| Ultimate Value Type | Protestant | Catholic | Jewish | None | Other |
|---|---|---|---|---|---|
| Religious optimist | 14 | −5 | −70 | −72 | −37 |
| Hopeful | 14 | −1 | −57 | −73 | −88 |
| Secular optimist | 9 | −22 | −32 | −1 | 36 |
| Pessimist | −22 | 12 | 78 | 110 | 65 |
| Diffuse | −12 | 10 | 82 | 37 | 41 |
| N = | (885) | (360) | (31) | (93) | (36) |

particularly overrepresented in any type although they are disproportionately missing from the ranks of the secular optimists.
The Jews, as we have seen before, are highly overrepresented in
the pessimistic and diffused categories. Those with no religious
affiliation have also been discussed before. The "other" category
of religious affiliation includes those who do not define themselves as either Protestant, Catholic, or Jew, but who do claim
some religious group. They differ from the "none" and the Jews
only in their overrepresentation among the secular optimists. It
may be that these people are humanists of varying descriptions
and as such have no specific reference to God, but do have a
religious identity.

From these data, we can formulate rough demographic profiles
of each of the belief types. The religious optimists are more likely
than the other types to be black, older, relatively low on income
and educational measures, and Southern Protestants. The hopefuls
are more likely to be women, middle-aged and in the middle
income bracket, of Scandinavian or Irish Catholic heritage, and
with the previously mentioned exception, Protestant. The secular
optimists are more likely to be men, older and with relatively low
incomes, of British or German heritage, and members of one of
the smaller sectarian churches. The pessimists are likely to also be
men, but younger and in the medium income group. They tend to
be highly educated, of Italian or Jewish heritage, live in the Northeast and not affiliated with either the Protestant or Catholic faiths.
Those in the diffuse type also tend to be young men with high
incomes who are moderately well educated. They are of Irish
Protestant, Italian, or Jewish descent, live in the Northeast and
claim either Jewish, agnostic, or sectarian religious affiliation.

This profile is not meant to be very exact, but rather simply picks out the high points in each table and summarizes them. Naturally there are some overlapping and inconsistencies. However, the fact that the typology is more or less congruent with a demographic description of the population gives us a foundation upon which to begin building. An individual's context in this society is a mix of many factors and influences. Some are explicitly known and are readily available to the researcher; others are not. Age, racial and ethnic heritage, economic position, sex, and other such traits can be viewed as limits or boundaries within which each of us must come to grips with reality. In coming to grips with reality, we actually create our own new reality which is very specific to us as individuals. The system of values which we apply during this process is always in a state of flux. They must not change too fast, nor must they be too rigid. These "ultimate values" are our way of making meaning out of potential chaos. As Berger and Luckmann have put it:

> Primary socialization thus accomplishes what (in hindsight, of course) may be seen as the most important confidence trick that society plays on the individual—to make appear as necessity what is in fact a bundle of contingencies, and thus to make meaningful the accident of his birth.[27]

We would expect that a typology of ultimate values would show some congruence with those limiting factors which impinge on our own reality-formation process. Data discussed in this chapter indicate that this is in fact the case. The ways in which people react to stressful situations are linked to observable social boundaries which should, theoretically, influence such reactions. This is an empirical indication that the typology constructed from the vignettes does tap into the ways in which people relate to the nature of reality as they truly believe it to be.

# NOTES

1. William C. McCready, "The Persistence of Ethnic Variation in American Families," in *Ethnicity in the United States* by A. M. Greeley, New York: John Wiley, 1974, pp. 156-176.

2. John S. Reed, *The Enduring South*, Lexington, Mass.: D. C. Heath, 1972, pp. 10-12, 31-32.

3. Sidney Verba and Norman Nie, *Participation in America: Political Democracy and Social Equality*, New York: Harper & Row, 1972, p. 96.

4. Formula for over- and underrepresentation of characteristics within a subgroup of the population:

$$PR = \frac{X_i - Y_i}{X_i} \times 100$$

Where: PR = Participation Ratio
$X_i$ = percentage of the population in social group
$Y_i$ = percentage of social group in category (ultimate value).

5. Henry B. Biller, *Fathers, Sex Roles and Children*, Boston: Beacon Press, 1971. William C. McCready and Nancy A. McCready, "Socialization and the Persistence of Religion," *Concilium*, Vol. 1, No. 9, New York: Herder & Herder, 1973.

6. Thomas Pettigrew, *The Negro Family in America*, New York: Harper & Row, 1968.

7. Dick Gregory, quoted in Pettigrew, ibid., p. 49.

8. T. Mahon, *Impossible Revolution*, New York: Doubleday, 1969, pp. 23-24.

9. See items 38A and 47 in Appendix A.

10. Norman M. Bradburn, *The Structure of Psychological Well-Being*, Chicago: Aldine Press, 1969.

11. Andrew M. Greeley and William C. McCready, "Does Ethnicity Matter?" in *Ethnicity in the United States*, by A. M. Greeley, New York: John Wiley, 1974, pp. 91-109.

12. Ibid., p. 104.

13. Ibid., p. 78.

14. Ibid., pp. 84-85.

15. Andrew M. Greeley and William C. McCready, "The Men that God Made Mad," in *That Most Distressful Nation*, by A. M. Greeley, New York: Quadrangle, 1972, pp. 166-168.

16. Andrew M. Greeley, op. cit. (1974), p. 85-86.

17. Ibid., p. 86.

18. Paul F. Campesi, "The Italian Family in the United States," in *Social Perspectives on Behavior* by Stein and Cloward, New York: Free Press, 1958, pp. 76-81.

19. Carolyn F. Ware, *Greenwich Village: 1920-1930*, Boston: Houghton Mifflin, 1935, p. 156.

20. Andrew M. Greeley et al., "Parochial schools and value oriented education," (working title) forthcoming. Mission, Kansas: Sheed & Ward (a subsidiary of Universal Press Syndicate).

21. Marshall Sklare, *American Jews*, New York: Random House, 1971, pp. 111-117.

22. Ibid., p. 112.

23. John S. Reed, op. cit., p. 9.

24. William Albig, *Public Opinion*, New York: McGraw-Hill, 1939, pp. 165, 169.

25. *1970 Census of Population, Vol. 1, Part 1, Sec. 1*. Washington, D.C.: Department of Commerce, June, 1973, p. 7.

26. John S. Reed, op. cit., p. 61.

27. Peter Berger and Thomas Luckmann, *The Social Construction of Reality*, New York: Doubleday, 1967, p. 135.

# Chapter 4

# FAMILIAL BACKGROUND AND

# ULTIMATE VALUES

The importance of the family unit for the socialization of the young does not need to be stressed in this report. Literature supporting familial influence on subsequent personality traits is voluminous.[1] Up to and including the present era there has been no better institution invented for the raising of the young. Given the importance of this intimate experience, it would seem most probable that the set of ultimate values we have been referring to as basic beliefs would be influenced by the events that occur within the family of origin. Whether or not an individual sees the nature of ultimate reality as benevolent should depend, to some degree, on how that individual's parents answered the same question. A person's interpretative scheme is not solely his own creation. A meaning system does not develop in isolation. Berger and Luckmann have described the socialization experience as a potential hoax designed to convince Man that reality has meaning.[2] Their description of the way in which reality is constructed by the individual has many convincing points. Everyone has been preceded by other individuals who have contributed their own interpretative schemes to the common heritage of the group, whether it be a family group or an ethnic group. Each subsequent meaning system draws on the common heritage for components. Each man stands on the shoulders of those who have preceded him and builds his own interpretative scheme on top of the legacies of his forebears.

Small children do not know what to make of the world around them. Will it harm them in some way? Can they count on those "big people" to keep coming home when they leave for the evening? Why must children always be so powerless just because they're smaller than everybody else? The young take their cues for the meaning of events from those around them. When the parents are happy and appear pleased with life, the children are happy. When the parents give indications that life is not very good and that there are insurmountable problems in the way of happiness, the children assumes that this is the way things "really are" and reacts accordingly. Some children react by trying to make reality change. Perhaps this means taking responsibility for an unhappy marriage or an ill parent. Other children will try to avoid the problem altogether by withdrawing into a world of their own making.

Psychiatric casebooks are filled with examples of the coping activities and strategies of children caught in a reality which they are not equipped to handle. For our present purpose, it is sufficient to note that the literature supports the position that one's interpretative plan or meaning system is formulated during early socialization and subject to later modification.[3] Biller's interesting work in the area of sex-role development indicates that boys do not get all their sex-role patterning cues from the father figure, but take them from any available source when the father is actually or psychologically absent.[4] He reports a case study which provides a poignant illustration of this process.

> Tony, a two year old, only lived with his family up until the age of eighteen months, and he saw his father very little. His actual relationship with his father was very limited, but Tony perceived himself as having an extremely close relationship with his father. He talked about his father doing everything with him and he attempted to emulate every detail about his father's behavior that he could remember.[5]

The point of this illustration is that if this boy can "construct" a father, to whom he had a very close and satisfactory relationship, he was taking cues about his own masculine role from an environment rather than from a real person. Cues as to the sensibility of ultimate reality were received in the same manner. In order for the communication of cues to occur, it is unnecessary to actually have close relationships within the family as long as the individual thinks that there were such relationships.

## Parental Social Class

Since these perceptions begin at an early age, we might hypothesize that reflections on one's familial background would provide useful information and insight into the nature of one's ultimate values. If we think of the familial world of the child as a microcosm that is preparation for the macrocosm that is the real world of the adult, it seems likely that the experience of the microcosm, and whether it was perceived as supporting or threatening, would influence the definition of the macrocosm as supporting or threatening. The variables to be used to examine this relationship are all retrospective responses given by the respondents concerning their parents' lives. They are respondent's perceptions which reflect their vision of the microcosm they lived in while their ultimate values were being formed.

The standardized scores in Table 4.1 for the parents' education levels indicate a relationship between parental education and the type of ultimate values held by the individual. Religious optimists tend to have mothers who are more than a quarter of a standard deviation below the mean level of education for the sample, while

Table 4.1: Standard Points for Parents' Educational Level by Ultimate Value Types

| Ultimate Value Type | Mother's Education | Father's Education |
|---|---|---|
| Religious optimist | −30 | −26 |
| Hopeful | 08 | 10 |
| Secular optimist | 04 | 00 |
| Pessimist | 12 | 13 |
| Diffuse | 05 | 00 |
| N = | (1,194) | (1,121) |

NOTE: Standard Points have a mean of zero and a standard deviation of one hundred.

the pessimists have mothers who are somewhat above the mean. The remaining types have mothers who are slightly above the mean of education. It is likely that parents with higher levels of education present a different view of the world to their children than those with lower educational levels. They have greater expectations for their children and tend to be more concerned with whether they are "doing the right thing" for their children in any set of circumstances.

Research on parental values has indicated that there are differences between the expectations of mothers for their children which vary with social class. Well-educated mothers are more likely to value consideration, curiosity, and happiness in their children, and mothers from the lower educational levels are likely to value obedience, neatness, and cleanliness in children.[6] Middle-class mothers tend to emphasize children's self-direction, while lower-class mothers tend to emphasize their conformity to external authority. Such differences in value orientation reflect differences in world views which are transmitted from parents to their children.

Given the intercorrelation between the mother's and father's educational level (.59), we would expect the relationship between the typology and father's education to be very similar to that for the mother's education. The religious optimists have fathers who are well below the educational mean, and the pessimists and hopeful have fathers above the educational mean. Kohn's research indicates that fathers' values for their children are generally in the same direction as mothers', only they tend to be more intensely so.[7] These data on the mother's and father's educational level support our contention that there is, at the least, a difference between religious optimism and the other types with regard to the value orientations and expectations of parents. The religious pessimists tend to have parents from the lower educational levels and therefore would tend to have been exposed to expectations stressing conformity to an external authority. The other types, particularly the pessimists and the hopefuls, would have had parents who stresset self-direction.

Self-direction, according to the research, is related to tolerance for the positions of others, while conformity is related to intolerance for nonconformity.[8] As we shall see in a later chapter, religious optimists tend to be more intolerant than the other types. The typology is therefore related to those factors in the socialization process which influence the individual's world view. However, we also know that one's own educational experience is very influential on one's values. What is the relationship between the respondent's educational level and that of his or her parents?

It is most likely that these variables work in tandem. People go on to higher education because they are motivated to do so by their parents, who have already experienced the process, and because they can afford to, which is also related to their parents' educational level. The crucial question in this cycle is whether specific ultimate values add to the motivation to succeed, or whether they result from having experienced success. Perhaps people are optimistic because they have never known failure or difficulties.

The first part of the question is reminiscent of the Protestant ethic dialogue of a few years ago. People of a particular value system desire higher education and therefore they are more successful than those who do not. The second part claims that the level of education an individual achieves influences his ultimate values. It is impossible with the present data to solve this dilemma, but we can shed some light on the matter. We would expect formal education to have little causal influence on membership in a particular type, since ultimate values are formed during primary socialization in the family and not during secondary socialization in schools. It is difficult to say whether education is the result of a world view or the cause of one; it is probably some combination of the two. However, there is evidence that those parents who choose to emphasize educational attainment to their children have a different view of reality than those who do not choose to do so.[9]

If we consider the father's educational level to be an indicator of his desire for educational attainment on the part of his children, we can test the effect of this emphasis on the creation of a system of ultimate values in the child. As can be seen in Table 4.2, the father's education has an effect only on the religious optimists and the pessimists. In all of the other types, the removal of the influence of the father's educational level has very little impact on the relationship between the respondent's education and his or her ultimate values.

Table 4.2: Standard Points on Educational Level Controlling for Father's Educational Level for Each Category of Ultimate Value

| Ultimate Value Type | Respondent's Education | Respondent's Education Net of Father's Education |
|---|---|---|
| Religious-optimist | −46 | −38 |
| Hopeful | 15 | 12 |
| Secular optimist | 00 | 02 |
| Pessimist | 20 | 10 |
| Diffuse | 15 | 13 |
| N = | (1,467) | (1,467) |

This means that well-educated fathers tended to reduce the propensity of the poorly educated respondent to be a religious pessimist and of the well-educated respondent to be a pessimist. For the other types, it did not matter very much whether their fathers were well educated; their own educational level is right around the mean for the population. The social environment in which a person is raised has a specified impact on his or her ultimate values. It is related to two of the types—pessimists and religious optimists—but it is unrelated to the others. This indicates that, although none of the types is totally influenced by environmental factors (as would have been the case if the father's education had erased the relationship between values and education), two of them are somewhat influenced by environment. Parental social position and the respondent's own social position, as measured by education, do not explain why people are hopeful, secularly optimistic, or diffuse in their values, but these two factors do link up with being pessimistic or religiously optimistic. Environment is more than educational level and social position, especially when we are considering its effects on values of a transcendent nature. The religious atmosphere of the family of origin must also be taken into account.

## Parental Religiosity

There are two indicators of religious atmosphere in this study. The first is the religious behavior of the parents, and the second is the approach of each of the respondent's parents toward religion. The relationship between parental religious behavior, as

Table 4.3: Standard Points for Parent's Church Attendance by Ultimate Value Types

| Ultimate Value Type | Mother's Church | Father's Church |
|---|---|---|
| Religious optimist | 13 | 15 |
| Hopeful | 15 | 16 |
| Secular optimist | 0 | −03 |
| Pessimist | −20 | −12 |
| Diffuse | −09 | −20 |
| N = | (1,416) | (1,379) |

measured by church attendance, and the respondent's ultimate values follows a predictable course. In Table 4.3 we can see that the church attendance of the parents of the religious optimists and the hopefuls is above the mean, that of the secular optimists is right on the mean, and that of the pessimists and the diffused is below the population mean.

In Table 4.4, we can see that the religious optimists considered both of their parents to have had a joyous approach to religion, while the hopefuls reported that their fathers were more likely to have such an outlook. The pessimists, and to a lesser extent the diffused, reported their parents to be well below the mean on this item. This item is intended to measure the quality of the religious atmosphere in the respondent's home while he or she was growing up. The actual question asked was:

When you were growing up, how would you describe your father's/ mother's personal approach to religion?

> Very joyous
> Somewhat joyous
> Not at all joyous
> Not religious

The response "not religious" was coded so that it did not count on the "joyous" scale. Fathers were generally rated as less joyous in their religiousness than mothers; twenty-four percent said their fathers were "very joyous," while forty-two percent placed their mothers in the same category. However, there is not very much difference between father and mother in Table 4.4. The only real difference at all is for the respondents in the hopeful type; their fathers are rated more joyous than their mothers. Given the mar-

Table 4.4: Standard Points for Parent's Approach to Religion by Ultimate Value Types

| Ultimate Value Type | Mother's Approach | Father's Approach |
|---|---|---|
| Religious optimist | 23 | 23 |
| Hopeful | 09 | 16 |
| Secular optimist | 04 | −04 |
| Pessimist | −24 | −25 |
| Diffuse | −10 | −08 |
| N = | (1,373) | (1,329) |

ginal distribution on this variable, it does seem likely that there is some quality about the fathers of those in the hopeful category which ought to be explored more fully.

Parental religiosity, as measured by church attendance and retrospective ambiance, does show a consistent relationship with the typology of ultimate values. The religious optimists, and to a lesser extent the hopefuls, have "religious" parents, in the rather strict sense of the word. The pessimists, and to a lesser extent the diffused, tend to have parents with low religiosity scores, and the secular optimists' parents are just about on the mean on both indicators.

The consistency of this relationship is all that is really important at this point in the analysis. The typology of ultimate values ought to coincide with other measures of religiousness in interpretable ways, and it does. We do not know for sure which way causality operates, but the association is quite clear. It may be that religious parents produce religious optimists, or it may be that religious optimists tend to remember their parents as being very religious people. We can speculate, at this point, that devotion and a sense of joy about one's religious affiliation would communicate hope and optimism to a child. The child would see his or her parents as members of an ongoing institution which would be there during the growing years and after. It is possible that this would formulate certain feelings of continuity and dependability within the child, which would then be converted to convictions about the hopeful future of humankind and the benevolent nature of ultimate reality. We can also ponder the possibility that, without institutional supports, the individual would be drawn more and more to a pessimistic stance regarding the ultimate questions surrounding the meaning of our existence.

These speculations do fit these data in a sensible fashion. It would be far more perplexing if we found that the pessimists had had very religious parents and those giving religious responses to the vignettes had had very nonreligious parents. For the purpose of establishing the credibility of the typology, all we need is the association between parental religiosity and the respondent's ultimate values—and that we clearly have.

## Affective Relationships

Religious perspective is not the only component of family atmosphere; there is also the affective dimension. A family consisting of four people—two adults and two children—has twelve dyadic relationships—i.e., mother to father counts as one relationship as seen by mother, and another relationship as seen by father. A large family, such as one with two parents and six children, has fifty-six possible dyadic relationships within its boundaries. Obviously there are some relationships which are more important to the family than others, and these receive more attention from the members of the family. A squabble between siblings is expected, tolerated, and frequently ignored, but a parental quarrel is much more important. Children are the best observers in the world. They seldom miss very much of what is happening around them. The quality of their parents' relationship is very important to the way in which they define the world. In her research on disturbed adolescents, Rita Stein documents some of the influences which parental relationships have on the growing child.[10] Numerous studies can be found which support the thesis that children are affected by the nature of their parents' relationship and how they, the children, perceive it.[11] One of the present authors had demonstrated a relationship between the happiness of the parents' marriage, as perceived by the children, and the children's religious devotion.[12] The implication of all of the above is that there is a connection between the way parents deal with each other and the way in which the children view the world.

One indicator of the quality of the parental relationship is how the respondent answered the question concerning the "closeness" between his or her parents. (This is question 15A of the survey.) In Table 4.5, we present the standardized score on this item for

**Table 4.5: Standard Points for Closeness of Mother and Father by Ultimate Value Types**

| Ultimate Value Type | Closeness |
|---|---|
| Religious optimist | 17 |
| Hopeful | −03 |
| Secular optimist | 01 |
| Pessimist | −12 |
| Diffuse | −01 |
| N = | (1,374) |

each of the types. There is slightly more than a quarter standard deviation separating the religious optimists from the pessimists, while the other three types are all very near the mean. Although we cannot determine the causal directions at this time, it is certainly plausible that there be a linkage between one's world view and one's view of the parental relationship. The credibility of the typology as an indicator of ultimate values is therefore enhanced by these data.

There are two other sets of questions which bear on this question of the association between relationship with one's parents and one's ultimate values. The first concerns how close the respondent felt he or she was to mother and father separately (survey items 15B and 15C). The second has to do with the respondents' feelings about how strict each of their parents was (survey items 15D and 15E).

We can see in Table 4.6 that a pattern similar to the one in Table 4.5 emerges. The religious optimists report that they were closer to both of their parents than the population mean, while the pessimists report that they were less close, especially to their fathers. The remainder of the types fall closer to the means for both variables. The reported levels of parental strictness, as can be

**Table 4.6: Standard Points for Closeness to Parents by Ultimate Value Types**

| Ultimate Value Type | Closeness to Mother | Closeness to Father |
|---|---|---|
| Religious optimist | 14 | 20 |
| Hopeful | 03 | 00 |
| Secular optimist | 00 | 08 |
| Pessimist | −09 | −18 |
| Diffuse | −09 | −02 |
| N = | (1,432) | (1,404) |

Table 4.7: Standard Points for Level of Parent's Strictness by Ultimate
Value Types

| Ultimate Value Type | Mother's Level of Strickness | Father's Strictness |
|---|---|---|
| Religious optimist | 22 | 23 |
| Hopeful | 05 | 02 |
| Secular optimist | −14 | −06 |
| Pessimist | −06 | −17 |
| Diffuse | −14 | −13 |
| N = | (1,433) | (1,401) |

seen in Table 4.7, are almost identical to the reports of parental
closeness. There is a slight variation, in that the secular optimists
report their parents to be a little less strict than the mean, particularly their mothers. Other than this, the data in these three
tables are remarkably similar.

The preceding measures of the quality of family life have the
same relationships with ultimate values. The religious optimists
see their families as having been close and disciplined; the hopefuls and the secular optimists come from families that were more
or less average in terms of closeness and discipline, while the
pessimists, to a lessor degree than the diffuse, come from families
which were neither close nor disciplined. One possible interpretation of these data is that the religious optimists are people who
feel close to the institutions of society. Just as parental church
attendance and approach to religion may communicate to the
child the availability of strong institutional support (Tables .4.3
and 4.4), so, too, closeness with and discipline in the family may
communicate that the family is a viable institution. The pessimists
and, to a lesser extent, the diffuse do not feel close to the institutions of either church or family.

### PARENTS AND PEERS

Another source of influence on one's ultimate values is the
instruction or information one receives from parents, friends,
school, and other inputs. A series of questions were asked under
an introductory statement:

Now I am going to read you some experiences that can influence a person's religious outlook, either toward religion or away from it. Please tell me, for each one, how important that was in influencing your own present feelings about religion—very important, somewhat important, or not at all important?

The responses were subjected to a factor analysis producing two factors, one representing parental influences and the other representing peer group influence. The items that clustered into the parental factor were:

Your parents' religious behavior. (16A)
Things your parents told you about God. (16B)
Your father's way of living. (16D)
Your mother's way of living. (16E)
General atmosphere in which you were raised. (16K)

The items that clustered into the peer group factors were:

Religious education in school. (16C)
Friends when you were in high school. (16F)
Friends after high school. (16G)
Your spouse. (16H)
Priests, ministers, rabbis, etc. (16I)
Some book(s) you have read. (16J)

In Table 4.8, we can see that parents had the greatest influence on the religious optimists and the hopefuls, while they had the least influence on the diffuse and the pessimists. These data indicate that while the respondents with more formally religious world views acknowledge their parents' contribution to that viewpoint,

Table 4.8: Standard Points for Parent's Influence on Religiousness by Ultimate Value Types

| Ultimate Value Type | Degree of Influence |
|---|---|
| Religious optimist | 25 |
| Hopeful | 18 |
| Secular optimist | − 03 |
| Pessimist | − 27 |
| Diffuse | − 28 |
| N = | (973) |

those who are less religious do not give the same acknowledgement to their parents, even though their parents tend to be less religious than average and logically should have some contribution to make (see Tables 4.3 and 4.4). In other words, parents are being credited with having some influence only when they themselves tend to be religious and only when their children are religious optimists or hopefuls.

The influence of nonparental figures, such as friends and schools, falls into the same pattern. In Table 4.9, we can see that the type which has ascribed most influence to these sources is the religious optimist, while the one which ascribed the least is the diffuse. Perhaps the most intriguing findings in these two tables is that the diffuse type reports the least amount of influence from both parents and friends. These people, the diffuse, have not chosen any consistent interpretation of the vignettes and are not willing to acknowledge the influence of either their parents or their friends on their religious outlook. These two facts are certainly congruent with each other, and together they paint a profile of a wandering meaning system which is unable to go in one direction. This is quite consistent with the theoretical description of diffusion.

Those respondents who can be called "religious"—that is, the religious optimists and the hopefuls, come together in these last two tables after having quite different responses to the items about closeness and discipline in the family. The interesting fact is that the hopefuls were no more likely than the average to say that their families were particularly close-knit or that their parents were particularly strict. Yet they are one-fifth of a standard deviation above the mean when it comes to assessing the influence

Table 4.9: Standard Points for Friend's Influence on Religious Perspective by Ultimate Value Types

| Ultimate Value Type | Degree of Influence |
|---|---|
| Religious optimist | 26 |
| Hopeful | 20 |
| Secular optimist | − 10 |
| Pessimist | − 19 |
| Diffuse | − 32 |
| N = | (973) |

their parents and friends had on their religious outlook. The religious optimists are consistent all the way along, reporting both close, highly supervised families and high parental and peer group influence.

The hopeful respondents are more likely to make a distinction, in this case, between the highly approved answers to several different items, and this is particularly important in the theoretical development of the typology. The whole idea of a hopeful type was that its members would not make the same general simplifications of reality that people with a more fundamental and literal conception of religion would make. The fact that the hopeful respondents did make a distinction between the description of their family atmosphere and the influences on their religious outlook, whereas the religious optimists did not, is very supportive of our hypothesis that these are two different ways of being nominally religious.

A final question in this chapter concerns the effect of education on the differences between these two types. We have seen that the religious optimists are the least well educated type and the pessimists are generally the best educated (Table 3.5). There is also a difference between the educational profiles of the two nominally religious types discussed in the previous paragraph. It may be that these previously mentioned differences are all due to the fact that the hopefuls are better educated than the religious optimists and are therefore more likely to make sophisticated distinctions.

We can see from a quick glance at Tables 4.10 and 4.11 that dichotomizing the respondents' educational levels does not alter the previously established patterns very much. The religious optimists, in both educational categories, are still above the mean

Table 4.10: Influence of Parent Controlled for Education

| Ultimate Value Type | Less than College | College |
| --- | --- | --- |
| Religious optimist | 26 | 18 |
| Hopeful | 24 | 08 |
| Secular optimist | 04 | − 14 |
| Pessimist | − 17 | − 41 |
| Diffuse | − 36 | − 18 |
| N = | (620) | (346) |

Table 4.11: Influence of Friend Controlled for Education

| Ultimate Value Type | Less than College | College |
|---|---|---|
| Religious optimist | 29 | 11 |
| Hopeful | 14 | 27 |
| Secular optimist | − 17 | 01 |
| Pessimist | − 17 | − 22 |
| Diffuse | − 27 | − 42 |
| N = | (620) | (346) |

in their estimation of both parental and peer influence on their religious outlook. Conversely, the pessimists and the diffuse are still well below the mean. The typology is obviously an indication of more than educational differences.

Education has the least influence on the religious optimists' rating of their parents' influence and on the pessimists' rating of their friends' influence. On the other hand, an increase in education depresses the estimation of parental influence for the hopefuls, while it raises their estimation of the influence of the peer group. Although there is some shifting around within each of the types, the important thing to conclude from these last two tables is that education does not account for the way in which these types have responded to these questions about the influences in their religious outlook.

## Conclusion

Ultimate values, or the way in which one conceives of ultimate reality, are clearly associated with familial factors and characteristics. People from more religious families tend to fall in one of the religious types, either religious optimism or hopefulness. On the other hand, these two types are divided as to parental education; the religious optimists come from rather poorly educated parents, while the hopefuls' parents are above the educational mean. The religious optimists report that they were closer than the average to their parents, and that their parents were stricter than the average. The critical point of these and other data is not what they describe, but rather what they mean.

At this point, we can say that three conclusions emerge from this chapter. First, there is a broad distinction between the two "religious" types and the remaining three types across several indicators of family milieu. Generally speaking, the religious optimists and the hopefuls group together, the pessimists and the diffused are at the opposite end of any specific measure, and the secular optimists are right on the mean.

Second, there are some interesting distinctions between the two nominal religious groups which serve to strengthen our claim that the vignettes are more sophisticated indicators of beliefs and values than previously used "religious" items, which were generally tied to orthodox theological or doctrinal positions. Last, there is a notable distinction between the impact of family or peer group on the respondents' religious outlook for the hopefuls when we account for the different educational levels within the group. Well-educated hopefuls are more likely to say that their secondary socialization experiences had the greatest impact on their outlook, while the less educated say that their parents had the greater impact.

Whether different socialization experiences actually cause different world views, we cannot say from these data. This question will have to wait until we examine the responses of parents and children from the same families later in this monograph. We can say that interpretable associations occur between family characteristics and the ultimate values typology. Religious optimists, and to some extent hopefuls, report positive influences from their families, and the pessimistic types tend to be negative, as we would expect. The next chapter will describe the relationship between the types and religious attitudes and behaviors. We would expect that those with a hopeful view of ultimate reality would be less likely to simplistically endorse the religiosity of their upbringing, and these data have supported that expectation. The religious optimists were rather simplistic in their reflections on their familial experiences, while the hopefuls were not. We would also expect that in the following chapter those of a hopeful persuasion would be more selective about their religious attitudes and behaviors than the religious optimists. If this is so, then the vignettes' ability to separate different conceptions of ultimate values will be quite difficult to deny.

# NOTES

1. M. Zelditch, Jr., "Family Marriage and Kinship," in *Handbook of Modern Sociology,* ed. by R. Faris, Chicago: Rand McNally, 1964, p. 490.

2. P. Berger and T. Luckmann, op. cit., p. 135.

3. Paul Musten, "Early Sex-Role Development," in *Handbook of Socialization Theory and Research,* ed. by David Goslin, Chicago: Rand McNally, 1969, p. 707.

4. Henry Biller, op. cit., p. 15.

5. Ibid.

6. Melvin Kohn, *Class and Conformity,* Homewood, Ill.: Dorsey Press, 1969, p. 31.

7. Ibid., p. 22.

8. Ibid., pp. 201-202.

9. Ibid., p. 34.

10. Rita Stein, *Disturbed Youth and Ethnic Family Patterns,* Albany, N.Y.: State University Press, 1971, pp. 184-195.

11. William J. Goode, E. Hopkins, and H. M. McClure, *Social Systems and Family Patterns,* New York: Bobbs-Merrill, 1971.

12. William C. McCready, op. cit., pp. 64-65.

*Chapter 5*

# ULTIMATE VALUES AND

# RELIGIOUS BEHAVIOR

This research enterprise began with the assumption that there are in American society different fundamental meaning systems that provide interpretation for ultimate reality. We assumed that such meaning systems are prior to religious behavior in two senses. First, they are chronologically prior in that they are absorbed at least in inchoate form in the very early years of life. They are also, it seems to us, logically prior in the sense that religious behavior, like prayer, contributes to an acceptance of creedal propositions and is conditioned by one's fundamental world view. For example, we would expect that the religious optimists would be devout churchgoers and that the pessimists would be quite nonreligious. The world view which displays confidence that God will take care of everything necessitates one's maintaining relatively close contact with God. On the other hand, a grim and angry world view either does not admit that there is a deity with whom to maintain contact or sees no point in dealing with such an ambiguous and enigmatic personage should he exist. The secular optimist, with "this worldly" expectations, will be somewhere between the religious optimist and the pessimist. The hopefuls, who take a more sophisticated and nuanced approach to the question of good and evil in the human condition, are likely to be less "religious" in the traditional sense than the religious optimists. because they may see less point in dealing with, pleading with, or placating the deity. It may be, however, that the hopefuls, with their complex vision of good and evil, might well be more religious than the religious optimists in some kinds of religious behavior, perhaps of the less traditional variety.

We commented facetiously at the beginning of this report that we were dealing with Greek, Egyptian, Mesopotamian, and Israelite belief systems, while the cultures that spawned them are long since dead. One must assume that the various interpretative schemes we have tentatively isolated with our belief typology are part of the overarching world view which we call, for lack of a better name, "Western." It is difficult to believe that very many Americans have ultimate value systems that are at great variance with the fundamental thrust of the two millennia of Western culture. Even the pessimists, for example, would have a hard time subscribing in the depths of their personalities to the life-denying and world-denying cosmic view so characteristic of many Eastern religions. We may have sorted out varieties of ultimate value systems within American society, but they still cluster around a fundamental Western world view. We suspect that the "life situation" items we designed for this study would have to be drastically modified if they were to be administered in cultures other than the North Atlantic.

This overarching world view in which we see ultimate value systems participating is a mixture of Hebrew, Graeco-Roman, and secular humanistic insights and is fundamentally optimistic, life-affirming, and world-accepting. We do not expect to find much trace of cultural despair in the American population.

We also expected that cross-tabulations and correlations between our ultimate value typology and, more explicitly, religious attitudes and behaviors would provide some sort of check, perhaps even a validation, of our use of the life situation vignettes to measure ultimate values. If those at the "religious" end of the typology are not more likely to be devout in the traditional sense and more confident of their religious convictions, there would be something wrong with our typology. If those toward the pessimistic end of the typology were not relatively "nonreligious" in the traditional sense, then one would have strong reason to question the typology. Finally, if there were not some rough correlation between the scales composed of the vignettes and the "fallback" scales composed of the much more conventional opinion items, the ultimate value typology would also be of dubious value.

However, we did not expect the complete absence of religiousness among the secular optimists or the pessimists. They participate in a Western culture which, in its American manifestation at least, endorses religion, and also the logical inconsistency between devotion and pessimism does not necessarily mean that the two are always psychologically incompatible. One can be angry at the universe and still go to church, and the reasons can range from "because everyone goes to church," "because my parents went to church," and "because there seems no special reason not to go to church," to "because going to church is consistent with being angry at the absurdity of the world."

## Developmental Perspective

We learned in the previous chapter that the religious types tended to see many different parts of their lives as influencing their perspective toward religion, while the nonreligious types— the secular optimists, pessimists, and diffuse—tended to see their perspective as developing independent of familial or peer group pressures (see Tables 4.8 and 4.9).

It is to be hoped that, at some time in the future, longitudinal research on the development of world views across time—say, from early high school years to the middle twenties—in order to determine how ultimate value systems change during the periods of adolescence and youth. Short of such indispensible, but prohibitively expensive, research, we must rely on retrospective questions, at best an unhappy compromise. Because of necessary limitations on the amount of time which could be spent on an interview, we had to be content in the present project with a question in which respondents were asked to place themselves on a "ladder" with ten rungs, saying how religious each was as a child, as an adolescent, and at the present time. The top of the ladder was the most religious; the bottom, the least religious. We also asked respondents to estimate where they expected to be on the ladder five years from now. The exact wording of the question was as follows:

Using the ladder, try to think of the *most religious* you think you could be and make that the top rung—10. Now think of the *least religious* you could be and make that the bottom of the ladder—0. Now, please tell me the number of the rung that represents:

A. Where you were as a child                0 . . . . . . . . . . . . . . 10

B. Where you were as an adolescent
   (teenager)                               0 . . . . . . . . . . . . . . 10

C. Where you are right now                  0 . . . . . . . . . . . . . . 10

D. Where you think you will be five
   years from now                           0 . . . . . . . . . . . . . . 10

The pattern of responses to this question is very revealing. Each of the types report that they were quite close to the mean on the religious ladder when they were children. The pessimists are the farthest away with —.12. By looking across the first row of Table 5.1, we can see that the extreme scores for the typology are separated by about one-fifth of a standard deviation when the point of reference is "childhood religiousness." However, this separation increases to almost a full standard deviation when the reference point is "the present" or "five years from now."

The information contained in Table 5.1 is presented graphically in Figure 5.1, and we can see that a very interesting pattern of religious self-description develops over time for each of the ultimate value types. The religious optimists begin slightly above the

**Table 5.1: Rating of Self on "Religious Ladder" by Ultimate Value Typology (standard points)**

| Ultimate Value Typology | Religious Optimist | Hopeful | Secular Optimist | Pessimist | Diffuse |
|---|---|---|---|---|---|
| As a child | 09 | 01 | 02 | −12 | 01 |
| As a teenager | 08 | 17 | 02 | −16 | −17 |
| Now | 30 | 43 | 02 | −46 | −33 |
| 5 years from now | 36 | 41 | 02 | −54 | −34 |

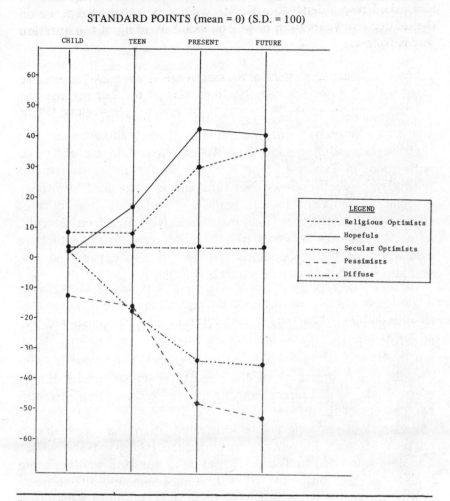

STANDARD POINTS (mean = 0) (S.D. = 100)

**LEGEND**
- - - - - - Religious Optimists
———— Hopefuls
-·-·-·- Secular Optimists
- - - Pessimists
·····-···· Diffuse

Figure 5.1: RELIGIOUS SELF-RATING ON "LADDER"

mean and increase during the period between adolescence and the present. The hopefuls, the other "religious" type, begin just about on the mean and increase right away. By the time they are in their teen years they consider themselves more religious than the religious optimists, and this lead continues. The secular optimists, to whom we would think religion would not be very salient, confirm this contention by never really getting off the mean at any time. The pessimists begin as far below the mean as the religious optimists are above it, and decline sharply, especially during the time between adolescence and the present. The diffuse begin at the same point as the hopefuls, but they move in the opposite direction almost immediately.

This pattern of responses is very exciting, because it verifies the theoretical interpretation of the typology. Each of the types behaves just as we would predict when asked about their religiousness retrospectively. They begin quite close together on this scale and sort themselves out, particularly during adolescence, into their various adult perspectives. When these data are combined with those in Tables 4.8 and 4.9, we get the impression that a religious perspective grows over time and is influenced by others, especially parents and friends, while a nonreligious perspective of the world develops over time, but is relatively free from parental or peer influences. At least it is free according to the subjective estimation of the respondents. We would also expect the two "religious" types to attend church frequently, just as they were more likely to describe themselves as more religious than the other types. Such an expectation is confirmed by Table 5.2. More than two-fifths of the religious optimists, and more than half of the hopefuls, go to church almost every week. Those at the "nonreligious" end of the typology are not completely absent from church; about one-third of the secular optimists attend almost every week, as do sixteen percent of the pessimists, and twenty-two percent of the diffuse.

As previous research has demonstrated, there is a very high correlation between the church attendance of husband and wife.[1] The data presented in Table 5.2 lead us to question whether there is also a correlation in ultimate values between spouses. This question is impossible to answer with these data. We must be content here with posing what strikes us as a fascinating problem: Do

Table 5.2: Church Attendance Almost Every Week or More by Ultimate Value Typology (in percentages)

| Ultimate Value Typology | Religious Optimist | Hopeful | Secular Optimist | Pessimist | Diffuse |
|---|---|---|---|---|---|
| Respondent | 42 | 54 | 31 | 16 | 22 |
| Spouse | 38 | 47 | 29 | 17 | 25 |

people with similar ultimate value systems seek one another out as prospective spouses, or does the force of the common life together lead to a convergence of ultimate values? It is to be presumed that both phenomena are at work, though, if we would be forced to guess in anticipation of further analysis, we would be inclined to think (mostly on the basis of McCready's research) that there is a tendency to seek out spouses of similar ultimate values, and that in cases of this similarity the wife will have more influence on the husband than vice versa.[2]

## Religious Behavior and Attitudes

Fifty-four percent of Americans pray every day and only four percent of the population never prays. This is a remarkable amount of praying, especially considering the fact that eleven percent of the population are sure that its prayers are not heard and thirty-one percent more are not absolutely confident that their prayers are heard. It would seem, then, that a good many Americans are praying "just in case," or "to whom it may concern," or because praying seem the thing to do regardless of whether anyone is listening or not, or perhaps because humankind, being what it is, finds it almost impossible not to pray.

In any case, the religious optimists are the most likely to pray every day (seventy-two percent) and the pessimists are the least likely. Still, almost one-third of them report that they pray every day. This is a fact worth emphasizing. The pessimists are those who see relatively little grounds for optimism or hope in life and are quite upset about the absurdity of human existence. Still, a third of them address some kind of communication to some deity every day of their lives—or at least claim to do so. But if you are a pessimist, why would you claim to do something like praying if you were not, in fact, praying? It may be that their pessimism only expresses part of a more elaborate and complex world view which still leaves room for dealing with a deity who, in the pessimistic perspective, can hardly be attractive. Or it may be that they pray regardless of who and what the deity is. It may even by that they pray for lack of something better to do, or that they might just as well touch all bases.

**Table 5.3: Frequency of Daily Prayer by Ultimate Value Typology (in percentages)**

| Ultimate Value Typology | Religious Optimist | Hopeful | Secular Optimist | Pessimist | Diffuse |
|---|---|---|---|---|---|
| All respondents | 72 | 71 | 56 | 32 | 41 |

The similarities between Tables 5.2 and 5.3 are not especially surprising. Those who believe that God will take care of everything are those who, almost as a matter of definition, are most likely to go to church and to pray. Those who reject either a simple divine intervention (in which the religious optimists believe) or a more complex one (in which the hopefuls believe) are the ones who would be the least likely to go to church and to pray. The similar responses, then, are perhaps little more than a matter of internal consistency, although in social research even internal consistency is something that can never be taken for granted.

Religion is not just a matter of devotions, as most authors on the subject have noted. One's religious perspective also involves the separation of reality into approximate categories of "sacred" and "profane." There ought to be some congruence between ultimate values and the way in which an individual defines these concepts.

The sacred is the "other," or the "totally other," the "tremendous," and the "fascinating." It is the opposite of the secular and profane. It is the collection of events and places in which the divine is perceived as "breaking into" ordinary events. The sacred is a theophany, a manifestation of the deity, and a "epiphany," a revelation of the Real. In subsequent chapters, we shall deal in some detail with the intense experience of the sacred which constitutes a mystical or an ecstatic experience. Here we shall content ourselves with an investigation of what sort of experience respondents define as religious—a sharing in some fashion in the sacred—and how they perceive themselves to be to God.

In one question, we asked our respondents what kind of activities they thought were religious:

|                                              | *Religious or Probably Religious* |
|----------------------------------------------|:---------------------------------:|
| (1)  Going to church services                | 89%                               |
| (2)  Giving money to the poor                | 76%                               |
| (3)  Thanking God for a promotion            | 67%                               |
| (4)  Visiting a sick friend                  | 62%                               |
| (5)  Listening to beautiful music            | 41%                               |
| (6)  Making love                             | 37%                               |
| (7)  Eating dinner with friends              | 26%                               |
| (8)  Demonstrating against the war           | 17%                               |

Eighty-nine percent of them thought going to church was religious, and thirty-seven percent thought that making love was, while only seventeen percent thought that demonstrating against the war was a religious activity. The items asked in question 17 fit themselves to a Gutman scale (see Appendix A). The properties of a Gutman scale are such that anyone answering the most indirectly related question positively (i.e., demonstrating against the war) is also likely to answer all the more directly related questions positively. Thus, those who think demonstrating against the war, eating dinner with friends, and making love are religious activities will, in all probability, consider going to church services, thanking God for a promotion, and giving money to the poor as religious.

A high score on this scale, which we have dubbed the "sacred scale," indicates that the respondent sees the religious in a wide variety of activities or situations. A low score indicates that one sharply distinguishes between the sacred and the profane and describes only a relatively limited number of activities as religious.

We might have expected that the religious optimists and the hopefuls would see the "presence of grace" as pervasive, while the secular optimists and the pessimists would try to sharply limit the domain of the religious. In fact, however, exactly the opposite turns out to be the case (Table 5.4). The hopefuls are most likely to delineate sharply between the sacred and the profane, while the pessimists are most likely to see religion everywhere. There are two possible explanations for this phenomenon. It may be that, since most Americans still consider religion a good thing, the pessi-

Table 5.4: "Sacred" Scale by Ultimate Value Typology (standard points)

| Religious Optimist | Hopeful | Secular Optimist | Pessimist | Diffuse |
|---|---|---|---|---|
| −17 | −26 | −09 | 31 | 23 |

mists wish to see it in ordinary secular activities. It may also be that the more traditionally religious have a narrower, and perhaps deeper, notion of what religion is, and find it necessary to distinguish sharply between the religious and the profane and the sacred and the secular. If one has a very deep reverence for the sacred, one may see it in fewer situations. If, on the other hand, one has little awe about the sacred, it may be easier to see it in quite commonplace and mundane activities such as eating and sex. The history of religions (as represented by such writers as Rudolph Otto and Mircea Eliade) has stressed a sharp distinction between the sacred and the profane that is much in keeping with the reaction of our hopefuls and religious optimists. On the other hand, a good deal of contemporary Christian theology has emphasized the pervasiveness of the sacred. (Karl Rahner has put it most succinctly: "Everything is grace.") This would seem to place contemporary theologians in the camp of the pessimists among our respondents.

The religious optimists and the hopefuls are also more likely to feel that they are closer to God and their churches than the three remaining types. In Table 5.5, we can see that they are both well above the mean for "closeness to God" and "closeness to the church." The secular optimists tend to be right on the mean for both indicators, while the pessimists and the diffuse are well below it. This pattern is very consistent with the ways in which each of the types answered the vignette questions, and it adds to the

Table 5.5: Closeness to God and to Church by Ultimate Value Typology. (standard points)

|  | Religious Optimist | Hopeful | Secular Optimist | Pessimist | Diffuse |
|---|---|---|---|---|---|
| God | 42 | 35 | −01 | −50 | −28 |
| Church | 42 | 32 | 02 | −48 | −33 |

evidence that the vignettes are in fact tapping into those ways in which people define and relate to the ultimate in their lives.

One of the critical questions with which we began our research was whether there would be a consistency between the scales we hoped to derive from life situation questions and the expression of religious opinions on "agree," "disagree" items of the more traditional survey research variety. After considerable experimentation and pretesting, we finally settled on eighteen "religious opinion items" which we thought might correlate in some rough fashions with the ultimate values we hoped to derive from our life situation questions. The eighteen items and the percentage of each of the ultimate value types giving a "religious" response are presented in Table 5.6. (The "religious" response may be agreement or disagreement depending on the wording of the particular question.) One can see from inspecting the table that in most cases the relationship between the ultimate value typology and the "religious" response to a question is both orderly and predictable. The religious optimists and hopefuls are the most likely to respond in the "religious" fashion, and the pessimists are least likely. However, there are a number of exceptions worth noting.

The first two items deal with purpose in life and survival after death and are particularly interesting because on both of these the hopefuls respond more vigorously than the religious optimists. We can think of two possible explanations. when one comes to such fundamental issues as purpose and survival, the capacity of the hopefuls to tolerate ambiguity leads them to be more inclined to be positive. They should be more likely to express confidence in both purpose and survival. Or it may simply be that the higher level of education of the hopefuls enables them to disagree with an opinion item that less sophisticated respondents accept uncritically.

There are three items—II, L, and P—in which there is little variation among the different ultimate value types. All of them, it seems to us, are items which represent the basic optimism of the overarching Western cultural world view. Being happy to be alive, accepting the daily problems as they come, and affirming life against the temptation to quit are powerful themes in the Western cultural tradition and represent some of the "common sense" to which most young Americans are socialized.

**Table 5.6: Agreement with "Religious Opinion" Items by Ultimate Value Typology (in percentages)**

| | Religious Optimist | Hopeful | Secular Optimist | Pessimist | Diffuse |
|---|---|---|---|---|---|
| A. Sometimes I am not sure there is any purpose in my life.[b] | 51 | 62 | 50 | 42 | 47 |
| B. Whatever happens after death the person that I am now will not exist any more.[b] | 30 | 34 | 26 | 14 | 19 |
| C. God's goodness and love are greater than we can possibly imagine.[a] | 91 | 92 | 78 | 52 | 58 |
| D. Despite all the things that go wrong, the world is still moved by love.[a] | 73 | 69 | 61 | 44 | 48 |
| E. God's love is not involved in anything that happens to us in this life.[b] | 68 | 79 | 54 | 36 | 50 |
| F. When faced with a tragic event I try to remember that God still loves me and that there is hope for the future.[a] | 88 | 87 | 69 | 42 | 53 |
| G. I feel that it is important for my children to believe in God.[a] | 96 | 94 | 82 | 63 | 71 |
| H. I would be happy to be alive even if death were the absolute end.[a] | 67 | 67 | 69 | 64 | 61 |
| I. There is more good in the world than bad.[a] | 56 | 62 | 60 | 45 | 51 |
| J. God encourages me to develop all of my potential abilities.[a] | 73 | 73 | 53 | 29 | 33 |
| K. God is passionately in love with me.[a] | 59 | 50 | 33 | 15 | 22 |
| L. The best way to live is to take the daily problems as they come and not worry too much about the big questions of life and death.[a] | 68 | 54 | 64 | 56 | 56 |
| M. There may be a God and there may not be.[b] | 75 | 85 | 61 | 41 | 46 |
| N. I believe in the existence of God as I define Him.[a] | 80 | 76 | 71 | 57 | 60 |
| O. I think that everything that happens has a purpose.[a] | 82 | 70 | 61 | 40 | 53 |
| P. Sometimes I look forward to death because life is hard.[b] | 57 | 66 | 62 | 68 | 68 |
| Q. I am not sure what I believe.[b] | 63 | 72 | 55 | 40 | 48 |
| R. Death may contain a pleasant surprise for us.[a] | 49 | 44 | 37 | 22 | 23 |

a. Agree strongly.
b. Disagree strongly.

In Clifford Geertz's catalogue of belief systems, common sense has an important place. It provides rough and ready answers to common, ordinary problems which do not challenge the ultimate interpretability of the universe. It may well be that the position represented by items H, L, and P are commonsense rather than religious values and should not be expected to vary with ultimate values. Furthermore, item I, which affirms that there is more good in the world than evil, does not vary as greatly among the first three types as do most other items, which suggests that for everyone but the pessimists and diffuse the notion that there is more good in the world than evil is a matter not of religious conviction but of common sense.

One other item which is interesting in and of itself is item G, which asks the respondent if he or she would want their child to believe in God. The point worth noting is not that the religious optimists and the hopefuls want their children to believe, for that goes without saying, but rather that two-thirds of the pessimists feel that it is important for their children to believe in God. Over half the pessimists say that they themselves believe in a deity, and, more than that, they want their children to do so. It would seem that being a pessimist does not preclude belief; it tempers and shapes it. God does exist for most of them, but He is incapable of changing the basically pessimistic nature of ultimate reality.

It is extremely difficult to examine so many attitude items one by one. Therefore, a factor analysis was performed on the items in Table 5.6, and four different scales were constructed. (For details of the factor analysis, see Appendix.) The "Faith" scale represents a dimension that asserts a fundamental belief in God's goodness. The "Survivor" scale loads positively on death containing a pleasant surprise and negatively on a cessation of existence with death. The "Common Sense" scale loads on those items previously discussed and seems to represent a commonsense cultural system rather than a religious cultural system. Finally, the "Agnostic" scale has strong loadings on items indicating the destruction of the human person after death, the purposeless of human life, the nonexistence of God, the nonpurpose of God's love, and uncertainty about what one believes.

We scarcely expect that there would be a perfect correlation between our types and our opinion scales. They approach questions of reality from a different perspective and deal with the complexities of basic belief with a different style. All we expected was that there would be a rough correspondence—though in the absence of such correspondence we would have been in deep trouble indeed. For example, the items in the Faith scale do not, by and large, seem to express a religious optimism that is quite so "easy" as the religious optimism that derives from the life situation questions. Still, we expected our religious optimists to score high on the Faith scale. Similarly, the Survival scale does not convey the same degree of ambiguity as do the hopeful items in our life situation questions. But we assumed that the hopefuls and the religious optimists would be inclined to be high on survival. Secular optimism as a basic belief system and common sense are not quite the same thing. But because there is so little transcendental content in the secular optimistic response, we thought it not unlikely that our secular optimists would fall back on common sense for dealing even with ultimate values, which for other people would transcend the boundaries of common sense. Finally, we expected a relatively strong relationship between secularism and pessimism, on the one hand, and agnosticism on the other.

Our expectations were sustained better than we had dared hope. As one can see in Table 5.7, the highest score on the Faith scale is attained by the religious optimists; the highest score on the Survival scale is attained by the hopefuls; the secular optimists are the highest on the Common Sense scale; and the pessimists are the highest on Agnosticism. The diffuse tend to be low on the Faith scale and about on the mean for the other scales.

The typology and those factor scales are derived from entirely different questions in our survey, and the fact that there is a con-

Table 5.7: Scores on Opinion Value System Scales by Ultimate Value Typology (standard points)

| | Religious Optimist | Hopeful | Secular Optimist | Pessimist | Diffuse |
|---|---|---|---|---|---|
| Faith | 50 | 38 | 04 | −57 | −34 |
| Survival | 23 | 28 | −02 | −35 | −14 |
| Common sense | −10 | −05 | 12 | 05 | 04 |
| Agnostic | 04 | −39 | 04 | 26 | 09 |

sistent and interpretable relationship between them is very encouraging. Since the vignettes and the typology derived from them are an innovation in survey research, the onus in this comparison is on them, and they seem to be as good as or better at tapping ultimate values than are the more traditional survey-type items.

The typology not only works, in terms of being related to the independent variables, but it is supported by theoretical underpinnings which are not present for the array of standard survey items. Respondents are asked to place themselves in quasi-real situations of stress. They are then asked for an interpretation of the situations which is related to some theoretical dimension of ultimate values, such as hopefulness. The only possible justification for using such an elaborate survey device is that it is a better predictor of the responses on the independent variables than some other device. We would argue that the differences between the religious optimists, the hopefuls, and the other three types more than justify the use of such an elaborate technique.

## Acceptance of Religious Propositions

Finally, we have attempted to discover whether our respondents accepted certain fundamental, nondoctrinal, propositions of the traditional Judeo-Christian world view; the survival of human beings; the primacy of the love of God; purpose in the universe; meaning in iniquities; and the efficacy of prayer. We asked if they agreed with these propositions and, if so, how sure they were in their agreement. These responses were then collected into five scales and standardized. (See Appendix A for the exact wording and the details of the scale construction.)

The scores for each of the types on these scales are presented in Table 5.8. Several facets of this table are worth noting. First of all, the religious optimists and the hopefuls differ rather dramatically on the first three propositions. The hopefuls are much higher in their certitude that man survives death and that the universe is not run by chance. The religious optimists, on the other hand, are higher in their belief that God's love is behind everything that happens. These are two different perspectives toward ultimate reality, which may both be legitimately named "religious." One type hopes in the future by focusing on survival and some kind of

Table 5.8: Attitude of "Very Sure" Toward Basic Religious Issues by
Ultimate Value Typology (standard points)

| Propositions | Religious Optimist | Hopeful | Secular Optimist | Pessimist | Diffuse |
|---|---|---|---|---|---|
| Man survives after death | 18 | 45 | −09 | −31 | −34 |
| God's love is behind everything that happens | 53 | 24 | 06 | −47 | −36 |
| The universe is not governed by chance | 02 | 20 | −08 | −09 | −09 |
| Meaning can be found in suffering and injustice | 21 | 24 | 09 | −36 | −14 |
| My prayers are heard | 41 | 41 | 12 | −57 | −37 |

divine purpose or guidance, while the other depends on the belief that God is always watching out for its interests.

Second, it is worth noting that the secular optimists are consistently close to the mean on these indicators, while the pessimists and the diffuse are consistently below the mean by a wide margin. The sole exception is the proposition that the universe is not governed by chance; only the hopefuls are off the mean by an interesting margin. It is likely that they are more sensitive to the issue of chance governing the universe, since they have more of a stake in hoping that it does not. The religious optimists do not need to worry about uncertainty, since they refer everything, rather simply, to God. The secular optimists are not particularly concerned about any of these propositions, and the pessimists and the diffuse are already convinced that existence is either malevolent and uninterpretable, so uncertainty is not an issue for them. It is an issue only in the value system of the hopefuls, and they are the only type who really express an opinion on the subject.

We constructed a Religious Certainty index from the items listed in Table 5.8, which gives respondents a high score if they are very certain of all of the five propositions. The religious optimists and the hopefuls are equally high on this index, as can be seen in Table 5.9, while the pessimists and the diffuse are well below the mean. Once again, the secular optimists are right around the mean for the index. The Religious Certainty index clearly discriminates between the ultimate value types—there is almost

Table 5.9: "Religious Certainty" Scale by Ultimate Value Typology (standard points)

| Religious Optimist | Hopeful | Secular Optimist | Pessimist | Diffuse |
|---|---|---|---|---|
| 40 | 39 | —03 | —50 | —38 |

an entire standard deviation separating the extreme types—as one would expect, since there is a logical relationship between one's ultimate values and one's certitude in basic religious propositions. Those with "religious" world views ought to be more certain about religious propositions, and indeed they are.

To summarize briefly the findings reported thus far in this chapter, we can see that the ultimate value typology does, in fact, relate to religious self-description, devotional behavior, closeness to God, and the distinction between the sacred and the profane in interpretable ways. It also relates strongly to a number of more traditional attitude measures of religiosity, as well as to certainty about a number of religious propositions. We can therefore conclude that our confidence in the typology derived from the vignettes is well placed. Ultimate values are a more sophisticated form of "religious" values, but they should be related to each other.

### MODELS FOR RELIGIOSITY

Finally, on measures of subtle religious attitudes or beliefs such as whether or not the world is run by principles of chance and whether or not people survive death, the hopefuls appear to be more "religious" than the religious optimists. A distinction between these two types is a key motive for developing the vignettes in the first place, since much of the previous research on religious beliefs has lumped all those giving "religious" answers together, when in fact they have different perspectives about the nature of ultimate reality.

We now turn to developing an analytic model of religious behavior in which we utilize the relationships we have been discussing. There will be four dependent variables in the model: confidence in the survival of the human personality after death

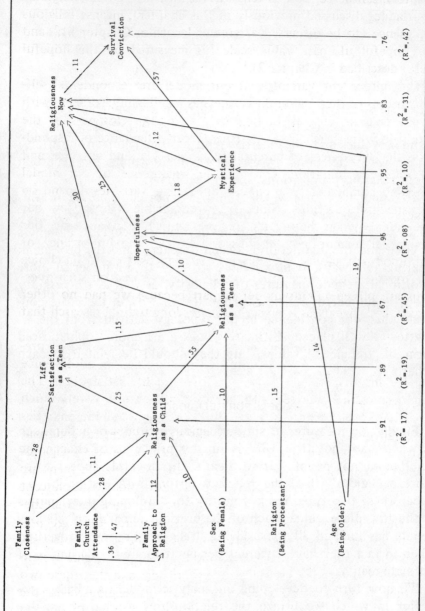

Figure 5.2: MODEL FOR SURVIVAL CONVICTION

(as measured by the survival factor described previously in this chapter); self-perception as religious (as measured by the religiousness ladder discussed previously in this chapter); intense religious experience (to be discussed at greater length in Chapter 8);[3] and the hopeful ultimate value scale (as measured by the hopeful factor described in Chapter 2).[4]

The antecedent variables on our model are respondents' self-perceptions of their own religiousness as a child and as a teen, with recollection of life satisfaction as a teen, the closeness of the family in which each grew up,[5] the church attendance of respondents, the joyousness of parental religious style, and sex, age, and religious denomination. One of the weaknesses of our model should be immediately apparent. Six of the variables depend on retrospective questions. Since we were unable to interview our respondents when they were teenagers and children, and since our theoretical assumptions heavily emphasized the importance of childhood and adolescent religious experiences, we had no choice but to ask retrospective questions. Variables based on such questions are placed in our model in part because we had no other choice, and in part as a prescription for longitudinal research that we are hopeful will be done at a later date.

There are two other weaknesses in the complex model presented in Figure 5.2. We assume that religiousness in adolescence is more an effect than a cause of adolescent life satisfaction. The religiousness that emerges in the teen years, we argue, is very much a result of a combination of childhood religion and the anxieties and challenges of teenage self-discovery. The theoretical argument is sound enough. However, the three measures we use (religiousness as a child, satisfaction as a teen, religiousness as a teen) are hardly adequate to measure the complexities of the late adolescent ideology crisis and the world view that results from it. Nonetheless, the three variables and the triangle in which they are presented can serve as a rough representation of the adolescent crisis.

Another weakness is that we assume that a hopeful value system predisposes one to intense religious experiences and that these two together predispose one to describe oneself as religious. That the value system may come before self seems to be a sound theoretical concept and that mystical experiences intensify religiousness also seems moderately plausible. However, one cannot exclude the

**Table 5.10: Zero-Order Correlations in Path Model in Figure 5.1 (only correlations .10 or above are given)**

| Item | Zero-order Correlation |
| --- | --- |
| *Religiousness as a Child* | |
| Parental religious joy | .18 |
| Parental church attendance | .37 |
| Family closeness | .22 |
| *Life Satisfaction as a Teen* | |
| Parental religious joy | .22 |
| Parental church attendance | .08 |
| Family closeness | .35 |
| Religiousness as a child | .32 |
| *Religiousness as a Teen* | |
| Parental religious joy | .24 |
| Parental church attendance | .31 |
| Family closeness | .22 |
| Religiousness as a child | .63 |
| Life satisfaction as a teen | .34 |
| *Hopeful Ultimate Value System* | |
| Parental church attendance | .13 |
| Sex (female) | .17 |
| Protestant | .16 |
| Religiousness as a teen | .12 |
| *Mystical Experience Several Times or Frequently* | |
| Parental religious joy | .11 |
| Parental church attendance | .10 |
| Family closeness | .11 |
| Religiousness as a teen | .11 |
| Hopeful ultimate value system | .21 |
| *Religious Now* | |
| Parental religious joy | .17 |
| Parental church attendance | .18 |
| Family closeness | .16 |
| Sex (female) | .11 |
| Religiousness as a teen | .36 |
| Hopeful ultimate value system | .32 |
| Mystical experience | .23 |
| Age | .27 |
| Life satisfaction as a teen | .18 |
| *Score on Confidence in Survival Factor* | |
| Family closeness | .16 |
| Parental religious joy | .18 |
| Parental church attendance | .19 |
| Religiousness as a teen | .17 |
| Hopefulness | .23 |
| Mystical experience | .62 |
| Religiousness now | .30 |
| Age | .11 |
| Denomination | .13 |

possibility that the hopeful ultimate value system could be more the result of intense religious experiences than a predisposing cause.

Finally, we postulate that there is a linkage between self-perception as religious and the conviction of human survival; one might argue—though we think less convincingly—that the causality should go in the opposite direction. However, the standardized correlation between these two variables is so small that the point may be moot. The causal linkage between mystical experience and conviction of survival is abundantly documented in the mystical literature.

We have laid out all the weaknesses of the model of Figure 5.2 because honesty and professional responsibility compel us to do so. But all social science models have weaknesses and limitations. The purpose of the model is not to describe reality perfectly or accurately, but simply to provide tools for more careful and detailed consideration of reality. We do not think it unreasonable to suggest that our model can be a useful tool, at least in pointing out what important questions remain to be answered.

Before turning to the model in Figure 5.2, the reader may wish to inspect the accompanying Table 5.10. The table presents the zero-order correlations (cf., .10 or above) of each consequent variable (that is to say, the variables to the right on the path diagram) with all its antecedent variables (that is to say, the variables to the left of the diagram). These zero-order correlations are what the relationship is between two variables when the influence of none of the other variables in the model is taken into account. Thus, there is, for example, a correlation of .23 between Hopefulness and confidence in Survival. There is, however, no direct path between Hopefulness and Survival on the model. This means that the standardized correlation (or beta coefficient)—the correlation when the effects of all the variables in the model are taken into account—between Hopefulness and confidence in Survival has declined to less than .10. In fact, in this case it has declined to .06. Hopefulness, in other words, only indirectly "causes" confidence in Survival; it is mediated through present religiousness and through mystical experiences. Similarly, life satisfaction as a teen influences self-perception as religious now (.18), but not directly. This influence is channeled through religiousness as a teen and for ultimate value systems. The reader who is interested in tracing the paths of influence may do so by comparing the zero-order coefficients on Table 5.10 with the standardized coefficients (or "betas") to be found on Figure 5.2.[6]

Turning at last to Figure 5.2, we can see that the family variables explain about a fifth of a person's retrospective estimate of how religious he or she was as a child. Furthermore, familial church attendance and familial religious joyousness influence religiousness as a teenager only indirectly through religiousness as a child and through life satisfaction as an adolescent. The only direct path between family background and adolescent life satisfaction comes from family closeness, which, incidentally, does not directly influence religiousness as a child, but does indirectly influence religiousness in adolescence. The whole family-childhood-adolescent system focuses on religiousness as a teenager, and all the influence these variables have further down the line is channeled through teenage religiousness. As was noted in Table 5.10, many of these variables influence present religiousness and confidence in Survival, but they do so indirectly through the religiousness of a person during adolescence.

Being hopeful is influenced by being a woman, a Protestant, and having a "religious" adolescence. Hopefulness, in turn, predisposes a person to have at least several mystical experiences.

Self-description as religious now is influenced by four direct paths: .3 from religiousness as a teen; .25 from the hopeful value system; .12 from frequent mystical experiences; and .19 from being old. (Whether this is a life cycle, generational, or a secular phenomenon is beyond our present competence to judge.) The more hopeful, the older, the more mystical, and those with a more religious adolescence are the ones who are most likely to describe themselves as religious now. But note that religiousness as an adolescent has both a direct linkage to present religiousness and indirect links through hopefulness and through hopefulness and mystical experience, while hopefulness in turn has a direct and indirect link through mystical experience. In other words, the various factors which combine to make one think of oneself as religious in adult life are linked together in a subtle and complex web. The fairly complicated set of lines, boxes, and numbers, as shown in Figure 5.2, is a horrendous oversimplification of reality.

Human religiousness in the real world is more complicated than our model, not less complicated, and this should be kept in mind whenever one is tempted to make any unidimensional explanation of religious behavior.

Perhaps the most interesting aspect of the model is the last step. Over two-fifths of the variance on the factor measuring confidence in one's survival is explained by the model.[7] (It perhaps should be noted that there are two items which have the strongest loadings on this factor: "Death may contain a pleasant surprise for us," and "The person that I am does not cease to exist after death.") Only a minor part of the successful explanation of variance is channeled to or originates in a self-description as religious. A substantial part of the variance in one's certainty about the survival can be explained by intense religious experiences. In brief, the zero-order correlation of .62 is only reduced by five points to a beta of .57 when all the other variables in our model are taken into account. Those who have been through an ecstatic interlude, it seems, have very strong feelings on the question of death containing a pleasant surprise.

For purposes of the present chapter, the principal function of Figure 5.2 is to show how the value systems "fit in" to a much more elaborate and complex explanation of religion. The values are shaped by childhood and adolescent experiences (as well as, in the case of hope, by sex and denomination). They, in turn, shape present religious attitudes and behavior, and apparently can predispose certain people to strong religious experiences which increase certainly in fundamental religious convictions. Ultimate values are a link between past experiences and present attitudes, behaviors, predispositions, and convictions about what the future might hold. To make such an assertion is, of course, nothing more than to restate the assumptions with which our project began. But now we can at least present the assumptions sustained by evidence that the relationships we thought were there do, in fact, exist.

# NOTES

1. McCready, op. cit., p. 46.

2. McCready, op. cit., p. 47. Himmelfarb, *Religious Socialization of Jews,* unpublished Ph.D. dissertation, University of Chicago, 1974.

3. "Religious" is used here with no reference to any denomination.

4. See pages ●-● in Chapter 2.

5. Item 15 in Appendix A.

6. Betas are standardized for the effects of all of the variables which precede them in the model.

7. The "$R^2$" is equivalent to the percentage of the variance explained. An $R^2$ of .42 means that forty-two percent of the variance is explained by the model.

*Chapter 6*

# THE RELATIONSHIP BETWEEN THE

# "QUALITY OF LIFE" AND ULTIMATE VALUES

## Life Satisfaction

The most common sociological approach to the subject of ultimate values or beliefs has been functional analysis. Religious beliefs were viewed as having a specific purpose within the personality, usually either adaptive or expressive. An adaptive function helped people change and adjust to the reality that they were finite and powerless in the cosmic sense. Weber regarded the problem of meaning that arose when death or suffering occurred to be the most salient example of the adaptive function of belief.[1] Humans are also regarded as having an expressive need which is satisfied by having a set of beliefs or values that allow them to act out their feelings toward the Ultimate Being.

Freud described religion as born of the need to make the helplessness of man tolerable.[2] The father of psychiatry felt that religion was an unsteady crutch, which was worse than no crutch at all. Empiricists as diverse as James and Jung concluded that religious beliefs had beneficial psychological results, and the dialogue continued.[3]

Contemporary psychologists have produced typologies that attempt to reconcile the divergent views concerning the utilitarian nature of belief. Allport relied on a distinction between intrinsic religious belief, which had an integrative function in the personality, and extrinsic belief, which provided the individual with some sense of security against unseen terrors.[4] More recently, Rokeach devised the open-closed polarization of belief, with an open mind being well adjusted and a closed mind being defensive and insecure.[5]

Finally, two psychiatrists, Lowe and Braaten, have linked believing with the ability to attain a social cathexis.[6] As patients receded from social reality, they tended to lose any emotionally charged interest in religion, and as they got well they regained a quality of cathexis within their religious experience.

Most theorists have viewed religion and religious belief as a mode of adaptation to stressful life events. The question remains as to whether it is emotionally healthy and mature to believe in some power outside oneself. Recent research into the correlates of psychological well-being has provided a methodology by which researchers can measure the relative levels of well-being within a population. This chapter will relate these measures to the typology of ultimate values.

Parcell Jahoda noted in 1958 that happiness was one of the criteria used in evaluating positive mental health.[7] Bradburn proposed a model based on the following proposition:

> A person's position on the dimension of psychological well-being is seen as a resultant of the individual's position on two independent dimensions—one of positive affect and the other negative affect. An individual will be high in psychological well-being in the degree to which he has an excess of positive over negative affect and will be low in well-being in the degree to which negative affect predominates over positive.[8]

Psychological well-being has been found to be associated with work and marital satisfaction, social participation, and social position. Several measures of well-being were included in our questionnaire, some from the earlier work of Bradburn, and some from the work of Cantril.[9] What is the relationship between well-being and ultimate values? We would expect the way in which individuals define ultimate reality to have some effect on how happy they felt, and how high a degree of well-being they experienced. If the types of basic beliefs are measuring real phenomena, the religious and secular optimists and the hopefuls should express a higher degree of well-being than the pessimists.

Hadley Cantril has developed a method for measuring one's level of satisfaction with one's own life at the present time as compared to some time in the past. This device is called "the self-anchoring striving scale," or the "ladder" scale.[10] A variation of this technique was used in Chapter 5 to test for religious self-description. The respondents were asked to rank themselves on ladders representing the quality of their lives at various times; childhood, adolescence, the present, and five years into the future. (The items are questions 21A through 21D in Appendix A.) The scores on the ladders were then converted to standard scores with a mean equal to zero and a standard deviation of one hundred.

These scores are shown in Table 6.1 for each of the value types. The religious optimists are slightly above the mean during their childhood, and they ascend to about ten points above the mean during adolescence and stay there. The hopefuls, on the other hand, begin at the highest level and remain there until they contemplate their future, when they rise once again. This perspective of looking to greater satisfaction in the future certainly seems to be compatible with hopefulness as a world view. The secular optimists steadily sink toward the mean until they think about their future, at which point they drop rather sharply below the mean. The pessimists start below the mean and stay there, although it should be noted that they think their future will be slightly better

Table 6.1: Standard Points for Life Satisfaction by Ultimate Value Types

| Ultimate Value Type | Satisfaction | | | |
| --- | --- | --- | --- | --- |
| | As a Child | As a Teenager | Now | 5 Years from Now |
| Religious optimist | 05 | 11 | 12 | 09 |
| Hopeful | 08 | 08 | 00 | 14 |
| Secular optimist | 06 | 03 | 01 | −15 |
| Pessimist | −13 | −16 | −21 | −16 |
| Diffuse | −06 | −08 | −02 | 05 |
| N = | | | (1,415) | |

than their present. "Nothing can be as bad as this," seems to be a reasonable attitude for a pessimist to assume. The diffuse wander above and below the mean and show a brighter perspective on the future than on the past or present.

Although the variations on the life satisfaction measures are quite small, they are all in expected directions. The pessimists are one-fifth of a standard deviation below the mean at present, which is the largest gap in the table. It appears as though one's ultimate values do have some influence on one's world view, although the causal direction is impossible to determine with these data. It is most logical that the level of satisfaction is influenced by world view, rather than vice versa, since the latter is theoretically the underpinning of the individual's perception of how things really are.

There may be a possibility that the respondents are telling us things they think we want to hear, that they are placing themselves in what they consider to be "the best light." What effect would this have on these questions about how satisfied they are with their lives—past, present, and future. We could hypothesize that there would be a considerable influence, since all these measures are subjective. In order to examine this question, we included in the survey selected items from the Crown-Marlowe Social Desirability scale.[11] The purpose of these items is to give the respondent a chance to admit that he or she has the same general flaws that most humans do, or to deny the fact. The specific items in our shortened version of the scale are contained in Appendix A, questions 10A through 10G. They cover such topics as whether or not one has ever disliked anyone, how well one gets along with obnoxious people, whether one gossips, and so on. The theoretical assumption upon which this measure is based is that we all do these things once in a while, and those who deny doing them are attempting to place themselves in the best possible light, therefore making themselves more socially desirable people.

The standard scores on our version of this scale are shown in Table 6.2 and are quite revealing. A high score indicates that the respondent is trying to present a particularly acceptable self-image. There is a good split on this scale in that the religious optimists are a third of a standard deviation above the mean, the pessimists are slightly farther below the mean, and the hopefuls

**Table 6.2: Standard Points on Social Desirability**

| | |
|---|---|
| Religious optimist | 31 |
| Hopeful | .03 |
| Secular optimist | 16 |
| Pessimist | −.35 |
| Diffuse | −.08 |
| N = | (438) |

are just about on the mean. If any of the types is trying to make themselves seem better it is most likely the religious optimists, and possibly the secular optimists. This indicates that the optimists, to some degree, are seeing themselves and possibly their world through "rose-colored glasses." Once again, the distinction between the religious optimists and the hopefuls indicates that these are two different religious perspectives and ought not to be lumped together when examining the correlates of belief.

### PSYCHOLOGICAL WELL-BEING

One of the questions Professor Bradburn found to be indicative of a person's psychological well-being was the single item asking how happy one was. This question also shows an association with the value types (Table 6.3). The pessimists have the lowest happiness score, and the hopeful people are as far above the mean as the pessimists are below it; they are the most happy of the five types.

A more detailed measure of psychological well-being devised by Bradburn is the positive-negative scale. The following items generate both scales; the odd-numbered items measure positive affect and the even-numbered items measure negative feelings.

**Table 6.3: Standard Points for Happiness Item by Ultimate Value Types**

| Ultimate Value Type | Happiness |
|---|---|
| Religious optimist | 02 |
| Hopeful | 15 |
| Secular optimist | 01 |
| Pessimist | −13 |
| Diffuse | −05 |
| N = | (1,459) |

We are interested in the way people are feeling these days. During the past few weeks, did you ever feel:

|  |  | Yes | No |
|---|---|---|---|
| 1. | Particularly excited or interested in something? | 1 | 2 |
| 2. | Did you ever feel so restless that you couldn't sit still long?........................ | 3 | 4 |
| 3. | Proud because someone complimented you on something you had done?.............. | 5 | 6 |
| 4. | Very lonely or remote from other people? .... | 7 | 8 |
| 5. | Pleased about having accomplished something? | 1 | 2 |
| 6. | Bored? ................................ | 3 | 4 |
| 7. | On top of the world? ................... | 5 | 6 |
| 8. | Depressed or very unhappy? ............. | 7 | 8 |
| 9. | That things were going your way?.......... | 1 | 2 |
| 10. | Upset because someone criticized you? ...... | 3 | 4 |

The affect-balance scale is created by subtracting negative affect from positive. Those who are above zero on the balance scale have a surplus of positive affect and those who are below zero have a surplus of negative affect.

The most important finding in Table 6.4 is that the hopefuls are more than one-fifth of a standard deviation above the mean on positive affect. They are also the highest type on the balance scale. All the other types are very close to the mean on each scale, indicating that it doesn't make very much difference for one's affect whether one is a religious optimist or a pessimist; however, it does

Table 6.4: Standard Points for Personal Affect Scales by Ultimate Value Types

| Ultimate Value Type | Negative Affect | Positive Affect | Balance |
|---|---|---|---|
| Religious optimist | − 03 | −11 | −06 |
| Hopeful | − 03 | 22 | 17 |
| Secular optimist | −11 | −04 | 05 |
| Pessimist | 07 | −06 | −09 |
| Diffuse | 09 | −05 | −10 |
| N = | (1,384) | (1,373) | (1,408) |

Table 6.5: Standard Points for Personal Affect Scales with the Effect of
Education Removed

| Ultimate Value Type | Positive Affect | Negative Affect | Balance Score |
|---|---|---|---|
| Religious optimist | −.01 | −02 | −.02 |
| Hopeful | .20 | .02 | 14 |
| Secular optimist | −.05 | 06 | −06 |
| Pessimist | −14 | .02 | −12 |
| Diffuse | −18 | −04 | −09 |
| N = | (1,384) | (1,373) | (1,408) |

make a considerable difference if one has a set of ultimate values
that can be described as hopeful.

Bradburn reported a positive relationship between educational
level and high positive affect.[1][2] It is possible that one's educational level is responsible for the association between hopefulness
and positive affect. In order to control for this possibility, it is
necessary to remove the effect of education while examining the
relationship between the affect scales and the belief types. The
standardized scores in Table 6.5 have been computed in such a
manner as to do just that. The finding remains that the hopeful
people have a high positive affect even when the effect of their
educational level is removed. The score dropped from .22 in Table
6.4 to .20 in Table 6.5. The hopefuls are also the only type above
the mean for the balance scale, controlling for education.

Another measure of psychological well-being that applies to
married people only is the degree to which they receive positive
or negative affect from their marriages. The same methodology
is used to measure marital affect as was used to measure personal
affect. A series of questions is asked concerning the kinds of
things that make people feel good about each other and the kinds
of things that make them feel bad about each other. These generate a positive scale and a negative scale. The negative is then sub-
tracted from the positive to form a balance scale. The items which
form these scales are in Appendix A, questions 18 and 19.

The standardized scores on the marital affect scales show a
different pattern than did the personal affect scales. The religious
optimists are slightly below the mean for negative affect and for
positive affect (see Table 6.6). The hopefuls and the secular optimists are just about on the mean for each of the scales, indicating

Table 6.6: Standard Points for Marital Affect Scales by Ultimate Value Types

| Ultimate Value Type | Negative Affect | Positive Affect | Balance Score |
|---|---|---|---|
| Religious optimist | −11 | −14 | 01 |
| Hopeful | −07 | 02 | 06 |
| Secular optimist | −06 | 00 | 03 |
| Pessimist | 24 | 08 | −10 |
| Diffuse | −01 | 08 | 05 |
| N = | (1,037) | (1,037) | (1,037) |

that for them ultimate values and marital affect are not related. The pessimists, however, are almost one-quarter of a standard deviation above the mean for negative affect, indicating that they feel they have rather unsatisfactory marriages. The pessimists are the only type with a negative score on the balance scale.

These scores were then subjected to the same test as the personal affect scores. The effect of the respondent's educational level was removed to see if the scores in Table 6.6 would fluctuate. Examining Table 6.7, we observe that the scores have changed very little from those in Table 6.6. The pessimists are still high on negative affect, and the balance scale reveals that they are still the only type with more negative feelings about their marriage than positive.

The relationship between the measures of psychological well-being and ultimate values can be summarized as follows. The religious optimists are very close to the mean on almost every measure. Their belief system does not appear to be related to their sense of well-being at all. The individuals with a hopeful basic

Table 6.7: Standard Points for Marital Affect Scales with the Effect of Education Removed

| Ultimate Value Type | Positive Affect | Negative Affect | Balance Score |
|---|---|---|---|
| Religious optimist | −06 | −11 | 04 |
| Hopeful | 01 | 01 | 00 |
| Secular optimist | 06 | 00 | 03 |
| Pessimist | 26 | 16 | −11 |
| Diffuse | 02 | −05 | −01 |
| N = | (1,024) | (1,024) | (1,043) |

belief system have the highest scores for positive personal affect of all the types. They are happier than most, with a high degree of psychological well-being. The secular optimists are very close to the mean, as are the religious optimists. Their beliefs appear to have very little to do with either their personal affect or their marital affect. They also have the most negative marital balance score. The diffuse have a low life satisfaction score and are very close to the mean on the other indicators.

## PERCEPTIONS OF OTHERS

Thus far in this chapter, we have discussed the respondents' feelings about themselves and their situation in life. How do they feel about other people, and do those feelings have any relationship to their basic beliefs? The respondents were asked three questions as to whether other people could be trusted, they were helpful, and they were fair in their dealings with others. To some extent, these are questions about the quality of human nature and how the respondents saw it in others.

Once again, there is a striking difference between the religious optimists and the hopefuls. The former tend neither to trust people nor th think they are helpful or fair, while the latter are just the opposite (Table 6.8). It appears that having a hopeful perspective about the ultimate enables one to feel a bit more kindly toward one's neighbor.

Why should people with a hopeful belief system have the highest personal affect scores and feel positive about human nature? The earmark of the hopeful person is that he or she refuses to be overwhelmed by the existence of the mystery of evil. Tragedies happen, to be sure, but they do not mean that the

Table 6.8: Standard Points for Feelings About Others by Ultimate Value Types

| Ultimate Value Type | Helpful | Fair | Trustworthy |
|---|---|---|---|
| Religious optimist | −11 | −11 | −24 |
| Hopeful | 18 | 14 | 18 |
| Secular optimist | 00 | 00 | 11 |
| Pessimist | −04 | −04 | −03 |
| Diffuse | −04 | − 02 | 03 |
| N = | (1,402) | (1,467) | (1,434) |

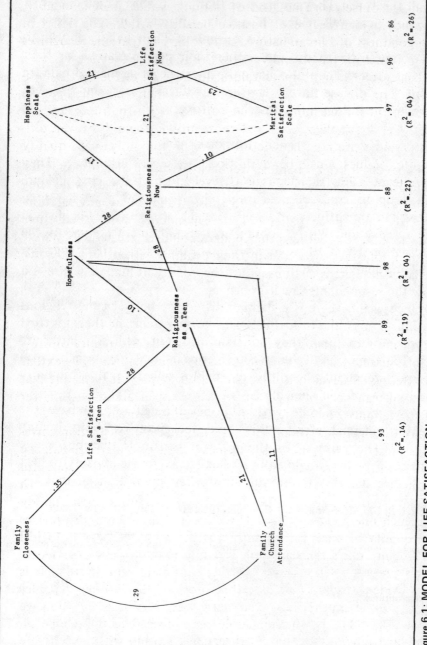

Figure 6.1: MODEL FOR LIFE SATISFACTION

universe has run amok or that we have been forgotten and left to fend for ourselves. This kind of outlook would, understandably, produce a high degree of positive personal affect. The belief in the goodness of human nature is a corollary in that one recognizes the evil that people do and yet sees the good that they are.

Basic beliefs or ultimate values do have an effect on the individual's quality of life. The interpretative scheme by which people understand the meaning of what happens to them influences how they feel about themselves and those around them. However, ultimate values are not the sole influence on the individual's quality of life. Values must, be definition, be subtle influences. They operate at a less than conscious level most of the time and are called up to consciousness only when events demant it. Many other factors influence the individual's sense of well-being and life satisfaction. We can obtain a more complete picture of the interaction of all these components if we bring them together into one analytical model.

## Models for Life Satisfaction

We must now raise the question of whether the quality of life— as measured by life satisfaction—can be explained to some extent by the model developed in the previous chapter. It turns out that a model can be developed which will explain about one-quarter of the variance on the life satisfaction scale (Figure 6.1).

We discover, first of all, in Table 6.9, that life satisfaction correlates positively with balance happiness (.33), with marriage balance (.34), with life satisfaction as a teenager (.24), with a hopeful ultimate value system (.10), with current religiousness (.31), with religiousness as a teen (.17), and with the closeness of the family in which one grew up (.16). Thus, the way in which one perceives the quality of one's present life is affected by one's psychological well-being, one's marriage, one's family in adolescent experience, one's present religiousness, and one's ultimate value system. It is also evident from Table 6.9 that most of these other variables relate to one another in a systematic way. The basic question we must ask, then, is whether adolescent life satisfaction, hopefulness, and religiousness have a direct relationship with present life

Table 6.9: Zero-Order Correlations in Last Two Steps of Path Model in Figure 6.1 (only correlations .10 or above are given)

| Item | Zero-order Correlation |
|---|---|
| *Balance Happiness* | |
| Parental church attendance | .22 |
| Parental religious joyousness | .26 |
| Family closeness | .10 |
| Religiousness as a teen-ager | .10 |
| Hopeful ultimate value system | .10 |
| Religiousness now | .20 |
| *Balance Marriage* | |
| Family closeness | .10 |
| Religiousness now | .13 |
| Life satisfaction as a teen-ager | .12 |
| Religiousness as a teen-ager | .14 |
| *Life Satisfaction Now* | |
| Balance happiness | .33 |
| Balance marriage | .34 |
| Life satisfaction as a teen-ager | .24 |
| Hopefulness | .10 |
| Religiousness now | .31 |
| Family closeness | .16 |
| Religiousness as a teen-ager | .17 |

satisfaction or whether they are channeled to such proximate influences on the quality of life as psychological well-being and a satisfactory marriage relationship.

One can conclude from Figure 6.1 that religion (at least self-perception as religious) has a direct impact on life satisfaction, as well as an indirect impact through its effect on psychological well-being and a satisfactory marital adjustment. Hopefulness affects both psychological well-being and life satisfaction through the medium of present religiousness, while family closeness, family church attendance, and adolescent experiences affect both psycological well-being and marital adjustment only through the media of hopefulness and current religiousness. One's ultimate value system and one's present religiousness are the channels by which childhood and adolescent experiences have an impact on the quality of one's present life.

## Conclusion

Whether one is hopeful or pessimistic does have an effect on the quality of one's life as measured by satisfaction, psychological well-being, and marital adjustment. People with hopefulness as an ultimate value tend to express above-average psychological well-being. On the other hand, people classified as pessimists tend to have poor marital adjustments and a history of being dissatisfied with their lives since they were very young. These two types of people have spun very different "webs of significance" for themselves. This chapter set out to test the effect of basic beliefs or ultimate values on the quality of life. Relationships have been demonstrated which offer strong evidence that the quality of life is dependent upon a set of factors, and that the ultimate value system of the individual mediates the influence of the background factors in such a way as to have a high degree of influence on the current level of life satisfaction.

# NOTES

1. Max Weber, *The Sociology of Religion,* Boston: Beacon Press, 1963, pp. 9-30.

2. Sigmund Freud, *Civilization and Its Discontents,* ed. by J. Strachey, New York: Norton, 1961.

3. H. B. Purcell, *Religion in Contemporary Cultures,* New York: Harper & Row, 1960, pp. 212-275.

4. Gordon Allport, *The Individual and His Religion,* New York: Macmillan, 1960.

5. Milton Rokeach, *Open and Closed Mind,* New York: Basic Books, 1960, pp. 347-365.

6. C. Lowe and R. Brooten, "Religious Attitudes in Mental Illness," *Journal of Social Science Research,* No. 3, Fall, 1966, pp. 435-446.

7. Bradburn, op. cit., p. 8.

8. Ibid., p. 9.

9. Hadley Cantril, *The Patterns of Human Concerns,* New Brunswick, N.J.: Rutgers Press, 1965, p. 103.

10. Ibid., p. 165.

11. D. Marlowe and D. P. Crowne, "Social Desirability and Responses to Perceived Situational Demands," *Journal of Consulting Psychiatry,* Vol. 25, 1961, pp. 109-115.

12. Bradburn, op. cit., pp. 90-92.

# Chapter 7

# ULTIMATE VALUES AND SOCIAL
# BEHAVIOR

Contemporary anthropologists distinguish between the concepts of "ethos" and world view. A people's ethos is the mood and quality of their life, while their world view is their idea of the way in which reality is comprehensively ordered. The meaning system which tells us how things, in their sheer actuality, really are, also tells us how the good person behaves if he or she is to integrate himself into the world. The relationship between ethos and world view is an essential component in all religions, because individuals need to have general principles with which to order their activities. According to Clifford Geertz, this is the basic characteristic of religion.[1]

> Whatever else religion may be, it is in part an attempt (of an implicit and firectly felt rather than explicit and consciously thought-about sort) to conserve the fund of general meanings in terms of which each individual interprets his experience and organizes his conduct.

Religions strive to tell their believers how to live in harmony with reality, as defined by the tradition, as well as describing the nature of the reality.[2]

> It is a cluster of sacred symbols, woven into some sort of ordered whole, which makes up a religious system. For those who are committed to it, such a religious system seems to mediate genuine knowledge, knowledge of the essential conditions in terms of which life must, of necessity, be lived.

The approved structure of reality and the approved style of living are taken to be in fundamental accord with one another, and this accord is a blueprint for integrated living.

Religion, then, is a systematic way of coping with ultimate reality. It provides answers to the most basic human questions which shape the perspective by which people view even the actions of daily life. World view confirms the appropriateness of ethos, and ethos confirms the credibility of the world view.[3] A natural question, then, is whether or not the typology of ultimate values has any relationship to the ways in which the respondents behave in social groups and the attitudes which they hold on social issues. We would expect that differences in world view, exercised through ethos, would have some effect on social behaviors and attitudes. Therefore, we would expect those in the various types, since ultimate values are "religious" in the broad sense, to possess different social attitudes and to exhibit different kinds of behavior.

The ability of the nominal variable "Religion" to predict attitudes is certainly open to question. As Ploch has observed, there are greater differences within most denominational groupings than there are between them.[4] This may be due to the fact that denomination does not signify differences in world view or ethos, and these are the variables which theoretically should influence attitudes and behaviors. Our typology, on the other hand, ought to reveal some attitudinal or behavioral differences precisely because of its link with world view.

Every survey project is forced to labor under constraints of time and finances. Ideally, we would have liked to have investigated the relationship between a wide variety of political, social and moral attitudes and behaviors on the one hand, and ultimate values on the other. Unfortunately, we could only address ourselves to a very limited number of social and moral questions. Another topic which we must save for different project is the process by which ultimate values are translated into attitudes and behaviors. Our present work is preliminary in nature, and many interesting leads will have to be left to future exploration.

There are undoubtedly some fundamental moral and social attitudes and orientations which are so much a part of Western culture as to cut across most value systems, though they may be more at home in some than in others. These would show little variation when sorted by our typology. However, there are more proximate social and moral questions for which the typology should be discriminating. We assume that ultimate values are not the only forces influencing these attitudes and behaviors, but that they are part of a complex and multifaceted system of influence that includes, among other components, another one of Geertz's meaning systems, ideology. An individual's social and moral attitudes will also be shaped in part by educational experiences, occupation, intelligence level, age, and, perhaps, ethnic heritage and region of residence.

In the "ideal world" (the subject of so many Sunday morning homiletic exhortations), there is an immediate and evident translation from ultimate values to proximate behavior and attitudes. However, in the real world inhabited by most people, the path from ultimate to proximate is more circuitous, obscure, and complex. This is so because reality is necessarily complex and the individuals making the journey along the path are unique. Therefore, we hypothesize that the relationships between ultimate values and proximate attitudes and behaviors will exist, but that it will be quite modest.

## Racial Tolerance

Since racism is assumed by many to be the most critical social and moral problem facing American society, we begin this chapter be investigation of the relationship between ultimate values and racial attitudes. The dependent variable to be used is NORC's racial integration scale, which has been used for over a decade to monitor changing racial attitudes in American society.[5] The items in the scale are questions 3G, 3H, 4, and 5 and they are listed in Appendix A.

The work of Gordon Allport and his colleagues led us to anticipate a correlation between religiousness and racism, for a specific kind of religiousness.[6] Allport demonstrated that those who were "intrinsically" religious—that is to say, they used religion for reassurance and peace of mind—were high on racist feelings. Those who were "extrinsically" religious—that is, they associated their religious feelings with concern for other people—were much less likely to be racist. In later research, it was discovered that the "indiscriminately" religious (those who agreed to both the intrinsic and extrinsic items on the scale) were the most racist of all.[7]

We were therefore not surprised at the results in Table 7.1. The religious optimists, perhaps roughly equivalent in their naivete to the extrinsically religious, are one-fifth of a deviation above the mean on the racism scale, while the other types are either on or just below the mean.

But, as was observed in an earlier chapter, the religious optimists are disproportionately from the South and from among the less well educated. We also know from previous research that Southerners and those who are less educated are more likely to score high on measures of racism.[8] Therefore, we asked ourselves to what extent the differences reported in Table 7.1 are the result of regional and educational variations between the different value types.

The racism scores of the Northern respondents are consistently lower than those for the Southern respondents, but in both the North and the South the religious optimists are the most racist. Among the Northern respondents, the hopefuls and the pessimists are the least likely to score highly on the racism scale, while among the Southerners that honor is shared by the hopeful, the

Table 7.1: Score on NORC Racism Scale[a] by Ultimate Value Typology (standard points on Gutman scale)

| Religious Optimist | Hopeful | Secular Optimist | Pessimist | Diffuse |
|---|---|---|---|---|
| 21 | −06 | 00 | −09 | −06 |

a. High score = racism.

Table 7.2: Racism Score[a] by Region by Ultimate Value Typology
(standard points on Gutman scale)

|  | Religious Optimist | Hopeful | Secular Optimist | Pessimist | Diffuse |
|---|---|---|---|---|---|
| North | 04 | −20 | −09 | − 21 | −14 |
| (n) | (256) | (182) | (119) | (82) | (123) |
| South | 48 | 20 | 20 | 28 | 21 |
| (n) | (207) | (56) | (30) | (17) | (28) |

a. High score = racism.

secular optimism, and the diffuse types. The respondents with that brand of religious world view we have labeled "hopeful" are among the least racist in both regions, and are clearly differentiated from the other religious world view we have labeled "religious optimism."

Region is not the only demographic factor that enters this discussion; educational level also makes quite a difference in the racism scores of individuals. As can be seen in Table 7.3, the respondents with less than a college education are all on or above the mean racism score, while all of those who at least attended college are below the mean. However, within each educational grouping there are interesting typological variations. For the less well educated and the better educated, the religious optimists are most racist. The hopeful and the pessimists have similar response patterns in that they are both well below the mean for the "college attendance" group, and in the middle of the distribution for the less well educated.

Table 7.3: Racism Score[a] by Education by Ultimate Value Typology
(standard points on Gutman scale)

|  | Religious Optimist | Hopeful | Secular Optimist | Pessimist | Diffuse |
|---|---|---|---|---|---|
| High school graduate or less | 27 | 10 | 11 | 11 | 01 |
| (n) | (200) | (114) | (103) | (58) | (83) |
| Attended college or more | −07 | −33 | −19 | −36 | −21 |
| (n) | (85) | (94) | (46) | (41) | (70) |

a. High score = racism.

**Table 7.4: Racism Score[a] by Ultimate Value Typology by Region and Education (standard points on Gutman scale)**

| Ultimate Value Type | North | | South | |
| --- | --- | --- | --- | --- |
| | High School | College | High School | College |
| Religious optimist | 08 | −13 | 57 | 03 |
| (n) | (198) | (57) | (92) | (28) |
| Hopeful | −08 | −39 | 42 | −21 |
| (n) | (107) | (75) | (37) | (19) |
| Secular optimist | −05 | −16 | 44 | −27 |
| (n) | (79) | (40) | (24) | (6) |
| Pessimist | −04 | −43 | 56 | −14 |
| (n) | (46) | (36) | (12) | (5) |
| Diffuse | −12 | −17 | 36 | −51 |
| (n) | (65) | (58) | (16) | (12) |

a. High score = racism.

Controlling for both region and educational level (Table 7.4) gives us a clearer insight to what is really going on with this variable. The religious optimists are the most racist in each of the four analytic categories. Among the Northerners, only the college-educated hopefuls and pessimists are more than two-tenths of a deviation below the mean for racism, while in the South it is the hopefuls, the secular optimists, and the diffuse who are well below the mean. The highest racism scores are from those respondents who live in the South and who have not been to college, and among this group, the diffuse, the hopefuls, and the secular optimists have the lowest standard scores.

The respondents with hopeful ultimate values are consistently lower on racism when we consider all of the analytic categories taken as a whole. This is congruent with our thesis that this world view is a specific kind of "religious" meaning system which ought to influence people to be more tolerant. Once again, the difference between the religious optimists and the hopefuls is very clear. Another interesting phenomenon is the great difference between the racism scores for the college-educated diffuse in the South as opposed to their less well-educated Southern counterparts. There are eighty-seven standard points separating these two groups, almost one standard deviation. Because the case bases are so small, it is difficult to be confident about the interpretation, but it may be that those Southerners with no specific ultimate value system (the diffuse) are more likely to have their racial attitudes changed by experiencing higher education than other Southern groups. College makes a great difference is about one-half a deviation, but it makes the greatest difference for the diffuse, perhaps because their attitudes are less well anchored in their meaning system.

In Table 7.5, we can see the same story told with a more sophisticated method. These scores are standard points on the racism scale, with the effects of region and educational level removed by a multiple regression procedure. It is abundantly clear that region and education attentuate the relationship between ultimate values and racism quite a bit, but even with these factors held constant, there is an eleven-point difference between the religious optimists and the hopefuls. The two "religious" world views are diametrically opposed with the fundamentalists being the most racist and the people who believe that good has a slight edge over evil being the least racist.

True, ultimate values do not tell the whole story by any means, but it is ironic that when the effects of the "sociological" variables, region and education, are removed, both the most racist and the least can be named "religious" people. The simplistic orientation to the nature of ultimate reality which is indicated by religious optimism demands that issues be either right or wrong, and actions be either good or bad. This kind of orientation makes it easy to see simple solutions to complex problems, and to find villains in social dramas. Prejudice is an easy answer to racial inequality. The more complicated orientation to reality, indicated by the hopeful responses to the life situations, deems it less likely that there are easy answers to anything human. Therefore, toler-

Table 7.5: Residual Racism Score by Ultimate Value Typology with Region and Education Removed

| Type | Residual Racism Score |
|------|----------------------|
| Religious optimist | 07 |
| Hopeful | −04 |
| Secular optimist | −01 |
| Pessimist | −02 |
| Diffuse | 00 |

ance is facilitated, and prejudice becomes an unacceptable answer to the problem of inequality in our society.

The remaining three types all cluster very near the mean for racism, indicating that a specifically "religious" world view is the only one which influences racial tolerance; one has a negative impact, the other a positive. Another segment of American life that is related to what one believes is the political stance one takes. Does the fact that a respondent is either an optimist or a pessimist have any influence on their political affiliation? The following section will deal with this and related questions.

## Political Affiliation

Politics has been connected with religion in American society from the first Puritan theocracy in New England to the present day. In more recent times, Protestants have been likely to be Republicans, while Catholics and Jews have maintained an uneasy alliance with the Democratic Party. There are also differences in the political styles of these groups, not just their party affiliation.[9] Recent analysis also shows that these groups are differentially resistant to the growth of political independence, with the Northern Catholics being the most likely to be Democrats, as they have always been.[10] Party identification is not unlike denominationalism in that once a person has chosen a party or a denomination the odds are that they will remain in that category. Most of the growth of political independence in recent years is the result of new people coming into the voting population who are not choosing to be Republicans or Democrats; it is seldom a matter of switching from either of the major parties to independence.[11] On the surface, there is no reason to expect to find a relationship between party affiliation and ultimate values, but if political choices are based on some inchoate system of beliefs about the way things are or ought to be, then there may be such a relationship. We can observe in Table 7.6 that there are indeed some very striking differences between the types in terms of their political affiliations.

The secular optimists are the most likely to be Republicans and the religious optimists are the most likely to be Democrats. The pessimists are the most likely to be Independents, which may be

Table 7.6: Party Affiliation by Ultimate Value Typology (in percentages)

| Ultimate Value Type | Republican | Democrat | Independent | Total |
|---|---|---|---|---|
| Religious optimist | 22 | 51 | 26 | 100 |
| Hopeful | 27 | 40 | 33 | 100 |
| Secular optimist | 33 | 37 | 29 | 100 |
| Pessimist | 22 | 40 | 38 | 100 |
| Diffuse | 28 | 42 | 30 | 100 |

their way of saying, "a plague on both your houses." The first question to raise is whether or not the traditional influence of the South on American politics is also responsible for these differences. In Table 7.7, we separate our respondents into those from the South and all others and ask for their party identification. The phenomenon of the secular optimists being Republican is a non-South one, as is the trait of the religious optimists being Democratic. In the South, the religious optimists are joined by the hopefuls and the diffuse as being highly Democratic, with the secular optimists not far behind. The only finding that carried over was that which said that the pessimists were most likely to be political Independents. This is true in both the South and elsewhere.

In Table 7.8, we have added the educational component to the analysis, and we consider the political affiliation of each of the types taking into account their educational level and region of residence. The religious optimists are most likely to be Democrats until we get to the well-educated non-South group, when they are likely to be either Independent or Republican. The secular optimists are more likely to be Democrats in the South, no matter what their educational level, and Republicans in the non-South, again regardless of education. The hopefuls are Democratic as long as they are not too well educated, regardless of region, and they

Table 7.7: Political Affiliation by Ultimate Values by Region (in percentages)

| Ultimate Value Type | South | | | Non-South | | |
|---|---|---|---|---|---|---|
| | Rep | Dem | Ind | Rep | Dem | Ind |
| Religious optimist | 25 | 51 | 24 | 21 | 51 | 28 |
| Secular optimist | 24 | 47 | 29 | 37 | 34 | 29 |
| Hopeful | 23 | 51 | 26 | 29 | 34 | 36 |
| Pessimist | 26 | 38 | 36 | 20 | 41 | 39 |
| Diffuse | 26 | 52 | 22 | 29 | 39 | 32 |

Table 7.8: Political Affiliation by Ultimate Values, Region, and Educational Attainment (in percentages)

| Ultimate Value Type | Low | | | | High | | | |
|---|---|---|---|---|---|---|---|---|
| | Rep | Dem | Ind | (n) | Rep | Dem | Ind | (n) |
| *South* | | | | | | | | |
| Religious optimist | 24 | 53 | 22 | (94) | 26 | 42 | 32 | (19) |
| Secular optimist | 22 | 48 | 30 | (40) | 28 | 44 | 28 | (18) |
| Hopeful | 18 | 62 | 20 | (76) | 33 | 28 | 39 | (36) |
| Pessimist | 26 | 47 | 26 | (49) | 25 | 25 | 50 | (32) |
| Diffuse | 16 | 64 | 21 | (44) | 57 | 14 | 29 | (14) |
| *Non-South* | | | | | | | | |
| Religious optimist | 18 | 57 | 25 | (159) | 38 | 22 | 41 | (32) |
| Secular optimist | 32 | 40 | 28 | (94) | 48 | 20 | 33 | (46) |
| Hopeful | 24 | 40 | 37 | (123) | 38 | 26 | 37 | (74) |
| Pessimist | 24 | 45 | 31 | (142) | 15 | 35 | 50 | (96) |
| Diffuse | 26 | 43 | 31 | (109) | 35 | 32 | 32 | (74) |

become predominantly Republican outside the South. The pessimists are also Democrats in the lower educational group, but just the opposite of the hopefuls, they become Independents when well-educated. The diffuse show a pattern entirely their own. In the low education group, regareless of region, they are Democrats. However, in the high education group, again regardless of region, they are Republicans.

For each type, low levels of education are indicative of membership in the Democratic ranks. It is only when dealing with the upper levels of education that some variation in this pattern begins to occur. Both kinds of optimists remain Democrats in the South, given a college education. Other than that, the types all move to another political position after college education is introduced. The pessimists become Independents in both the North and the South, and the hopefuls become Independents in the South, but split in the North. This is all by way of demonstrating the relationship between ultimate and political values. Obviously much more work could be done, especially since we are not really measuring political "values" but party identification which is associated, but different. However, there is clearly a relationship between the way in which people define the nature of the really real, and the kinds of political self-images they have. Future research on the political beliefs of people might find an examination of their ultimate beliefs or values quite worthwhile.

## Trust and Authoritarianism

We have now seen that there are complex relationships between both racial and political attitudes and the typology of ultimate values. Now we will turn to the question of whether or not certain other social attitudes are also related to these values. First of all, we investigated the possibility that one's ability or willingness to trust other people was influenced by one's ultimate value system. Our measure of trust was composed of three questions:

Would you say that most of the time people try to be helpful or that they are mostly just looking out for themselves?

Generally speaking, would you say that most people can be trusted or that you can't be too careful in dealing with people?

Do you think most people would try to take advantage of you if they got the chance or would they try to be fair? (See Appendix A for the detailed responses.)

Interestingly enough the largest difference on the trust scale is between the two "religious" types, the religious optimists and the hopefuls. In Table 7.9, we can see that there are forty-four standard points, almost one-half a standard deviation, separating these two groups. The secular optimists are slightly above the mean, and the remaining groups are right around the mean. It is also interesting that the pessimists are not more below the mean than they are. One would expect them to display little confidence in the trustworthiness of their fellows.

Table 7.9: Score on Authoritarian Scales by Ultimate Value Typology (standard points)

| Ultimate Value Type | Liberal | Conservative |
| --- | --- | --- |
| Religious optimist | 25 | 40 |
| Hopeful | −13 | 03 |
| Secular optimist | 00 | 05 |
| Pessimist | −01 | −31 |
| Diffuse | −14 | −15 |

Another way of looking at these data is to consider this a measure of the way the respondent considers the nature of human beings. Are humans basically good and worthy of being trusted, or are they basically evil and deserving of suspicion? The two religious perspectives' differences on this point are exactly what one would expect them to be. Those with the optimistic "God-will-take-care-of-everything" attitude are most likely to think that humans are weak and untrustworthy, while those with a "God-triumphs-but-its-going-to-be-close" kind of perspective are much more likely to trust their fellows and to think kindly of them.

The Authoritarian Personality scale has become part of the collective wisdom of social research. In its original form, it was roundly criticized because it supposedly measured authoritarianism of the right and not of the left. We have used what has come to be known as the "California F Scale," which purports to measure liberal and conservative authoritarianism.[1][2] Three items are intended to tap into conservative authoritarian attitudes:

People can be divided into two classes: the weak and the strong.

Strong discipline builds strong character.

There is hardly anything lower than a person who does not feel a great of love, gratitude, and respect for his or her parents.

These items were coded with the standard Likert-type agree-disagree responses. Three more items, coded the same way, were administered to tap into authoritarian attitudes with a left bias.

Faith in the supernatural is a harmful self-delusion.

Sex crimes, like rape and child-molesting, are caused by a sick society instead of guilty individuals.

To be a decent human being, follow your conscience regardless of the law.

As can be seen in Table 7.10, there is not really very much difference between these varieties of authoritarianism when it comes to the ultimate value typology. The religious optimists are the most authoritarian on both scales, which is congruent with their responses on the previous scale about human nature. If humans are not trustworthy, then it only stands to reason that

**Table 7.10: Score on Role of Women Scale<sup>a</sup> by Ultimate Value Typology (standard points)**

| | |
|---|---|
| Religious optimist | −18 |
| Hopeful | 02 |
| Secular optimist | 02 |
| Pessimist | 11 |
| Diffuse | 03 |

a. High score = progressive.

they ought to be watched and controlled. The pessimists are the least authoritarian on the conservative scale, and the hopefuls and the diffuse are the least authoritarian on the liberal scale. Once again the difference between the hopefuls and the religious optimists appears.

## Role of Women and Sexual Morality

Finally we presented our respondents with five questions about the roles of men and women in our society. We assumed that one's ultimate values would influence the way in which one perceived these important social roles. The five questions are listed in detail in the appendix, but they are listed here without marginals for the sake of comparison. (The response categories are Likert-type agree-disagree.)

A pre-school child is likely to suffer emotional damage if its mother works.

A wife should respond to her husband's sexual overtures even when she is not interested.

If a wife earns more money than her husband, the marriage is headed for trouble.

A husband should respond to his wife's sexual overtures even when he is not interested.

Parents should encourage just as much independence in their daughters as in their sons.

These items were put together into a scale which we will call the "Role of Women" scale. In Table 7.11, we can see that there is about a third of a standard deviation separating the religious

Table 7.11: Residual Scores for Social Attitudes with Education and Region Removed by Ultimate Value Typology (standard points)

| Ultimate Value Type | Progressive Role for Women | Liberal Authoritarian | Conservative Authoritarian |
|---|---|---|---|
| Religious optimist | −06 | 02 | 19 |
| Hopeful | 07 | −12 | −06 |
| Secular optimist | −01 | 01 | 05 |
| Pessimist | 05 | 03 | −14 |
| Diffuse | 06 | 04 | −22 |

optimists and the pessimists. All the other types are right around the mean.

However, we know that education and region influence these kinds of attitudes very much. We cannot claim any particular influence for ultimate values unless these two important factors are accounted for. In Table 7.12, we can see that the standard points for each of the scales we have been discussing change when education and region are controlled. Only the hopefuls are above the mean on trust; all the rest have moved toward the mean by wide margins. The religious optimists have remained well above the mean on the conservative authoritarianism scale, while the hopefuls are the only type below the mean on the liberal authoritarianism scale. There is not very much difference between the types on the Role of Women scale; none is more than seven points away from the mean. The hopefuls and the diffuse are the most progressive of all.

Controls for education and region, while greatly attenuating some of the relationships, have generally failed to eliminate the findings that social attitudes are indeed influenced by ultimate values. The most striking differences are those between the religious optimists and the hopefuls. They are all the more striking

Table 7.12: Moral Attutides by Ultimate Value Typology (in percentages)

| Ultimate Value Type | Premarital Sex Always Wrong | Approve Abortion Defective Child | Approve Abortion Want No More Children |
|---|---|---|---|
| Religious optimist | 57 | 78 | 28 |
| Hopeful | 51 | 76 | 31 |
| Secular optimist | 36 | 86 | 48 |
| Pessimist | 18 | 86 | 60 |
| Diffuse | 28 | 88 | 55 |

because these two types are at least nominally "religious." We would expect the pessimists to have different response patterns from those with more optimistic world views, and indeed they do. However, we might not expect those with variations on the same religious theme to have such differing ultimate value systems, yet they do.

The religious optimists appear to have a concept of the nature of people which clearly dichotomizes that nature into a good and a bad portion. People need to be controlled, cannot be trusted, and are divided by racial differences. The hopefuls, on the other hand, are much more moderate in their view of human nature. There is both good and bad at the same time and in the same person. You cannot divide the two parts and come up with easy answers to problems. The diffuse and the pessimists are well below the mean for the conservative brand of authoritarianism, but they are just slightly above the mean for the liberal version of the same attitude.

Our life situation items have shown an association with specific social attitudes in a manner consistent enough to enable us to say that they are measuring the ways in which the respondents are interpreting ultimate reality. The world views of the religious optimist and the hopeful are quite different from each other and from that of the pessimist. Differences are limited by education and region of residence, but they underlie both of these factors. If, as we suspect, the typology is reflecting ultimate value systems, the preceeding data in no way deny this, and even offer moderate confirmation.

The final topic in our discussion of the relationship between ultimate values and social attitudes is a moral one. Two of the most often-discussed moral issues are premarital sexual experience, and abortion. These are central issues in many of the moral codes and religious doctrines of our day. Our expectations would be that the religious optimists and the hopefuls would be traditional in their approach to these questions, and the remainder of the typology would be more progressive—i.e., in favor of them. Table 7.12 confirms these expectations. There are wide variations among the types with regard to the morality of premarital sexual behavior and the approval of abortion for purposes of birth control. There is much less variation on the subject of abortion in the case of a defective child. The religious optimists and the hopefuls are somewhat surprising in their support for this latter proposition. They distinguish sharply between the two abortion questions. There is a twelve percentage point spread in the first question and a thirty-two-point spread in the second one. It is clear that, at least on this issue, the religious optimists and the hopefuls are not guilty of a "knee-jerk" response, but contour their reactions to the specific situation.

These differences ought not to be interpreted as indicating that there is a direct linkage between ultimate values and attitudes toward sexual morality and fetal life. It is much more probable that there is an intervening variable at work, perhaps a traditionalism which inclines the religious optimists and the hopefuls to support those values which they feel are in keeping with the Western Christian tradition. Ultimate values will indeed influence moral choices, but through a circuitous, indirect route. Geertz is quite correct: ethos and mythos are flip-sides of the same coin. However, the way in which one flips the coin depends very much on the social context within which one finds oneself. The way ultimate values are linked to proximate attitudes depends upon such variables as educational level, region of residence, one's denominational heritage, one's ethnic heritage, and most probably a number of other complicating and intervening factors. To chart out the web of linkages between ultimate values and proximate attitudes may be even more difficult than to create indicators which enable us to measure, however crudely, the ultimate values themselves.

## A Model for Trust

Our goals in this chapter are more modest than were those in the previous two. We shall use a relatively simple model to determine whether ultimate values serve as a link between the background variables and trust. We have chosen to use trust as our dependent variable because of its implication for one's definition of human nature. If one sees people as being trustworthy, then one betrays a benign view of human nature.

We note that in the correlations of Table 7.13 the nonwhites and the "agnostics" are low on trusting their fellows, while the better educated and those with high psychological well-being

Table 7.13: Zero-Order Correlations Used in Model in Figure 7.1

| Item | Zero-order Correlation |
|---|---|
| *"Agnostic" Ultimate Values* | |
| Nonwhite | .13 |
| Educational attainment | −.18 |
| | |
| *Balance Happiness* | |
| Agnostic ultimate values | −.26 |
| Nonwhite | −.09 |
| Educational attainment | .13 |
| | |
| *Trust Scale* | |
| Nonwhite | −.24 |
| Educational attainment | .21 |
| Agnostic ultimate values | −.15 |
| Balance happiness | .21 |

score higher on trusting. We also note that nonwhites have higher scores on agnosticism and lower levels of education. Finally, these two groups are lower on happiness, while the well-educated are higher on the psychological well-being scale. To what extent are agnosticism and psychological well-being the channels through which socially disadvantaged respondents are led to distrust? We could ask this question in the reverse—that is, "to what extent are positive religious values the channels between 'whiteness' and higher educational levels on the one hand, and trust on the other?" However, the former exposition proved to be the neatest of the possible models.

Figure 7.1 shows that the relationship between being nonwhite and trust vanishes as a direct path. Nonwhites are less trusting because they are more "agnostic" about the purpose of human life, and consequently have lower scores on psychological well-being. There is also an indirect link between education and trust that runs through ultimate values and psychological well-being; but, unlike the racial path, education has a direct relationship with trust and an indirect one passing through happiness. The connection between race and trust is entirely indirect, through ultimate values and psychological well-being.

Education has both an indirect, as described above, and a direct influence on trust. Higher education leads to higher trust both

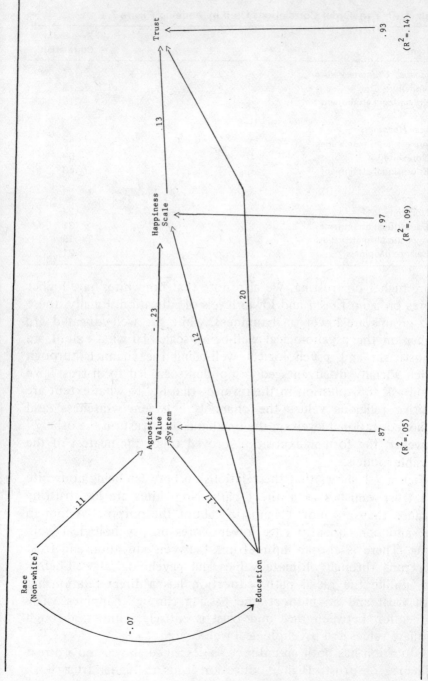

**Figure 7.1: MODEL FOR TRUST**

because it lowers agnosticism and increases happiness and because of a direct impact unmediated by either values or well-being.

The relationship between ultimate values and social attitudes is complex and indirect. The values can be influenced by such basic demographic factors as race and education. They, in turn, can influence the state of mind, such as psychological well-being, ultimate values can serve as a link between demographic factors and social attitudes. Only a modest fourteen percent of the variance in trust is explained by the model in Figure 7.1, but, as we noted, we did not expect very large correlations in this chapter. Our model does present evidence that mythos influences ethos; that the way in which people think things really are influences the way they think things ought to be, and ought to be done. Ultimate values, world view, basic beliefs, whatever we call these things, they do influence practical ethical decisions. Those who, for whatever reasons, reject the idea that human life is without meaning and purpose are likely to be happier people. And because they are happier, they are more likely to trust their fellows. It almost sounds like a conclusion of a Sunday sermon, but how many Sunday sermons are based on data gathered from the respondents in a national sample of the country?

# NOTES

1. Clifford Geertz (1973), op. cit., p. 127.

2. Ibid., p. 129.

3. Ibid., p. 127.

4. Donald R. Ploch, "Religion as an Independent Variable: A Critique of Some Major Research," in *Changing Perspectives in the Scientific Study of Religion*, ed. by Alan Eister, New York: John Wiley, 1974, p. 290.

5. A. Greeley and Paul B. Sheatsley, "Attitudes Towards Desegregation," *Scientific American*, December, 1971, pp. 13-19.

6. Gordon Allport, "The Religious Context of Prejudice," *Journal for the Scientific Study of Religion*, Vol. 5, Fall, 1966, pp. 447-457.

7 Gordon Allport and Michael Ross, "Personal Religious Orientation and Prejudice," *Journal of Personality and Social Psychology*, April 1967, pp 432-442.

8. Recent research has suggested that the correlation between education and racism is almost entirely a function of response set. That is, the better educated have lower scores on racism scales because their greater sophistication enables them to give the correct (nonracist) answers, not because their attitudes are any different from those of the less well educated.

9. Sidney Verba and Norman Nie, op. cit., pp. 97-101.

10. John Petrocik, *Changing Party Coalitions,* unpublished Ph.D. dissertation, University of Chicago, 1975.

11. Norman Nie, Sidney Verba, and John Petrocik, *The Changing American Voter,* Cambridge, Mass.: Harvard University Press, 1976.

12. Bernard M. Bass, "Authoritarianism or Acquiesence?" *Journal of Abnormal Psychology,* Vol. 51, 1955, pp. 616-623. I. J. Chapman and Donald T. Campbell, "Response Sets in the 'F' Scale," *Journal of Abnormal Psychology,* Vol. 54, 1957, pp. 129-132.

*Chapter 8*

## ULTIMATE VALUES AND THE PARANORMAL

We have a fantasy that takes place in what must be considered the capital building of American social science. A gentleman with a faintly Edwardian air enters with a manuscript and announces to a group of assembled scholars that he wishes to apply for tenure at their university. Looking up from last Sunday's *New York Times Book Review* and temporarily suspending their dreams of an office in the White House basement, the scholars leaf through the chapters briefly and shake their heads. "We are sorry, Professor James, but this 'Varieties of Religious Experience' is not a serious, scholarly work. We could not possibly consider you for a position on our faculty."

The point of the parable (and a good parable-teller should not have to explain the point) is that contemporary American social science may name its buildings after William James, but it is not much interested in doing research on the ecstatic experiences about which James' most famous work was concerned.

Outside the parapsychological literature, there is nothing in the way of systematic research on psychic phenomenon.[1] Anthropologists study mystical ecstasy in primitive and non-Western societies mostly from the point of view of the social and psychological "functions" of ecstatic experience. At one time, psychiatrists devoted their free hours psychoanalyzing the great mystics of the past (who were unfortunately not available for office couches). Despite the physical absence of the objects of interest, psychiatrists like Karl Menninger (in one of his early manifestations) were inclined to write off the mystics as self-punitive madmen and madwomen. "Hysteria" was the most frequent diagnosis.

Recently psychologists have become somewhat more benign about mystics, particularly that wing of the profession that flits in and out of the margins of the counter culture. Mystics, we are told, are not mad. They may be "like" schizophrenics; their experiences may be "like" regression; but a little of schizophrenia and regression in our "sick" society may be a good thing for you. It may be a way of breaking out of a serious personality crisis.[2] Maslow has a much more positive view of the "core religious" variety of peak experience. He did not find it at all necessary to speak of it as though it were "like" schizophrenia or "like" regression.[3]

One must search extensively through the sociological literature to find even the slightest hint that there is such a thing as a mystical experience. Bourque and Bourque and Back studied "transcendental experiences."[4] Laski, as an amateur, did an intelligent study of a nonrepresentative sample of friends and acquaintances.[5] Ennis wrote a theoretical article on ecstatic experiences.[6] Beyond these works, however, sociologists seem to be uninterested in the subject. Ennis notes, however, that most of the idols to whom sociologists burn incense (Marx, Freud, Weber, Durkheim, Mannheim) were aware of the phenomenon of "oceanic" experiences. Our own poking and probing among our colleagues would suggest that not all of them are insensitive to the existence of the paranormal or the mystical in their own lives. Still, it seems fair to say that the generally implicit assumption among orthodox social scientists is that ecstasy may be interesting if you are concerned with drugs or the counter culture, but it is not sufficiently widespread in American society to justify the collection of systematic data on the subject. If one is studying Bali, then of course one would be interested in ecstasy; but in the United States of America? Hardly.

Let us make the assumptions of our own research clear:

(1) We are prepared to take ecstatic individuals at their word that their experience is cognitive. They assure us that they *see,* that indeed they see things the way they *really are.* It is up to the psychologists of perception to determine just what perceptual phenomena are involved (and they should tell us on the basis of research, and not a priori reasoning). It is up to the philosophers and theologians to tell us whether what the ecstatics think they see really is the way things are. We are interested in the correlates, the antecedents, and the consequences of such an experience. We assume that the experience will have antecedents and consequences, whether the mystical experience is a breaking through to the ultimate reality or is merely a psychotic episode.

(2) We would define the ecstatic experience as religious. It is not religious in the formal ecclesiastical or doctrinal sense, but in the sense that religion has been defined by Luckman and Geertz:[7] a set of symbols that purports to provide a unique interpretive scheme to explain the ultimate reality. Mystics are "religious" whether they go to church or not, whether they profess any doctrine or not, because they claim to have seen and to know the way things *really are.* Their cognition in the ecstatic interlude is religious cognition in the sense that it is a cognition of the ultimate order of things.

(3) Like all experiences, the ecstatic interlude has its antecedents in the respondent's past. Since we have defined it as a religious experience in the Geertzian and Luckmannian sense, we also assume that the ecstatic experience, like all religious phenomena, will be strongly influenced by the relationships among the triad of mother, father, and child in th infancy, childhood, and adolescent years.[8] It will be affected by the quantity and quality of the religious life of the parents.

(4) We also assume that there will be consequences in attitudes and behavior from such experiences, at least for those who have them frequently. "Ethos" as Geertz remarked, "is the flip-side of the coin of mythos."[9] Our notions of how one ought to behave are direct consequences of our convictions about the nature of the cosmos in which one finds oneself constrained to behave. If the ecstatic experience is as powerful as those who have experienced it claim, there seems every reason to assume that at least those who

Table 8.1: Mystical and Psychic Experiences in a National Sample of Americans (in percentages)

| Questionnaire Item | Never in my life | Once or twice | Several times | Often | I cannot answer this question |
|---|---|---|---|---|---|
| *DEJA VU* Thought you were somewhere you had been before, but knowing that it was impossible | 38 | 29 | 24 | 6 | 3 |
| *ESP* Felt as though you were in touch with someone when they were far away from you | 40 | 26 | 24 | 8 | 2 |
| *CLAIR-VOYANCE* Seen events that happened at a great distance as they were happening | 72 | 14 | 8 | 2 | 4 |
| *CON-TACT WITH DEAD* Felt as though you were really in touch with someone who had died | 70 | 16 | 8 | 3 | 2 |
| *MYS-TICAL ECSTASY* Felt as though you were very close to a powerful, spiritual force that seemed to lift you out of yourself | 61 | 18 | 12 | 5 | 3 |

N = (1,467)

Table 8.2: Mystical and Psychic Experiences of Americans by Age (percentage ever)

| Age | (n) | Deja Vu | ESP | Clair-voyance | Contact with the Dead | Mystical Ecstasy |
|---|---|---|---|---|---|---|
| Teens | (54) | 87 | 69 | 49 | 31 | 32 |
| 20s | (388) | 80 | 59 | 26 | 23 | 33 |
| 30s | (253) | 70 | 58 | 20 | 21 | 33 |
| 40s | (246) | 55 | 56 | 21 | 27 | 38 |
| 50s | (288) | 57 | 62 | 29 | 33 | 43 |
| 60s | (184) | 38 | 58 | 26 | 40 | 36 |
| 70s | (113) | 38 | 64 | 28 | 39 | 35 |
| Average | | 61 | 60 | 25 | 30 | 36 |

have such experiences frequently will be different in some fashion in their values and behavior from those who do not.

(5) Finally, we assume that—and here we have the evidence of the Bourque and Back research—that ecstatic experience is not all that infrequent in American society. That social science does not examine a phenomenon does not compel us to conclude that the phenomenon does not exist.

One can approach this enterprise with alternative sets of hypotheses culled from the disorganized and impressionistic literature on the subject:

(1) The ecstatic is an oppressed, unhappy, rigid person who is looking for reassurance and release, which an interlude of self-induced withdrawal provides.

(2) The ecstatic is one who has had a "peak experience" that unleashes, however temporarily, the most creative and generous human resources.

Our own sympathies, perhaps because of our religious backgrounds (but also because of the ecstatics we interviewed), are more with the second hypothesis. But we are not so partisan as to ignore data supportive of the first.

The first five tables summarize the overall findings of our research on psychic and mystic experiences. Later, we shall focus on the mystical experience itself. We note in Table 8.1 that fifty-nine percent of our sample have experienced deja vu, fifty-eight percent have had ESP experience, twenty-four percent reported a clairvoyant experience, twenty-seven percent have been in touch with the dead, and thirty-five percent have "felt as though they were very close to a powerful spiritual force that seemed to lift them out of themselves." (Our carefully worded and thoroughly pretested question was distilled from the literature on mysticism and paranormal experiences.)

Young people are more likely to experience deja vu than old people (Table 8.2). The young and the old seem more likely to experience ESP than the middle-aged. Clairvoyance is more frequent among adolescents, but then it does not vary with age. Contact with the dead is most frequent among teenagers and among those over fifty. Mystical ecstasy is higher among those in their forties and fifties than among the rest of the population.

Table 8.3: Mystical and Psychic Experiences of Americans by Religious Affiliation (percentage ever)

| Denomination | (n) | Experience | | | | |
| | | Deja Vu | ESP | Clair-voyance | Contact with the Dead | Mystical Ecstasy |
|---|---|---|---|---|---|---|
| Protestant | (889) | 58 | 62 | 27 | 30 | 43 |
| Catholic | (361) | 59 | 52 | 23 | 26 | 24 |
| Jew | (29) | 76 | 71 | 23 | 32 | 29 |
| Other | (98) | 84 | 64 | 18 | 40 | 45 |
| None | (46) | 78 | 59 | 20 | 18 | 29 |

There is no evidence shown in Table 8.2 to suggest that there is a mystical revival going on among the young; rather, the phenomena seem widespread among all age levels in the population.

Mystical ecstasy (Table 8.3) occurs most frequently in the Protestant and "other" denominations and slightly more frequently among Jews and those with no religion than among Catholics. (If you have Canon Law and an infallible pope, perhaps you do not need a John of the Cross.)

One might expect that, within the Protestant denominations, mystical experiences would be most frequent where religious enthusiasm and emotionalism are most welcome. However, it turns out (Table 8.4) that the serene, stately Episcopalian denomination is most likely to have members who report having had a mystical experience. Episcopalians, incidentally, are also the most likely to report deja vu, extrasensory perception, and contact with the dead.

Table 8.4: Mystical and Psychic Experiences of American Protestants by Denomination (percentage ever)

| Protestant Denomination | (n) | Experience | | | | |
| | | Deja Vu | ESP | Clair-voyance | Contact with the Dead | Mystical Ecstasy |
|---|---|---|---|---|---|---|
| Baptist | (282) | 55 | 60 | 30 | 28 | 43 |
| Methodist | (181) | 59 | 60 | 21 | 32 | 40 |
| Lutheran | (101) | 59 | 59 | 27 | 28 | 37 |
| Presbyterian | (74) | 59 | 66 | 28 | 27 | 46 |
| Episcopalian | (35) | 89 | 80 | 18 | 44 | 50 |
| Other | (173) | 57 | 64 | 29 | 35 | 47 |
| No denomination | (40) | 67 | 62 | 29 | 21 | 52 |

**Table 8.5: Religio-Ethnicity and Psychic and Mystical Experiences (percentage ever)**

| Religio-ethnic Group | (n) | Experience | | | | |
|---|---|---|---|---|---|---|
| | | Deja Vu | ESP | Clair-voyance | Contact with the Dead | Mystical Ecstasy |
| *Protestant* | | | | | | |
| British | (167) | 67 | 65 | 23 | 30 | 45 |
| German | (131) | 61 | 59 | 21 | 24 | 37 |
| Scandinavian | (47) | 45 | 61 | 18 | 21 | 34 |
| Irish | (72) | 55 | 62 | 25 | 31 | 51 |
| American | (87) | 57 | 55 | 35 | 24 | 40 |
| *Catholic* | | | | | | |
| Irish | (47) | 57 | 48 | 17 | 25 | 38 |
| German | (48) | 62 | 48 | 25 | 15 | 19 |
| Italian | (52) | 65 | 45 | 26 | 30 | 25 |
| Polish | (43) | 51 | 65 | 26 | 34 | 18 |
| Spanish-speaking | (33) | 54 | 45 | 25 | 34 | 15 |
| Jew | (28) | 75 | 70 | 24 | 33 | 27 |

Maybe the English Richard Rolle and Juliana of Norwich had more influence than anyone realized.

Among the various American ethnic groups, the Irish—long noted as a fey, mystical people—seem to be the ones most likely within their religious affiliations to report mystical experiences. It is also worth noting that the Poles and the Jews, two ethnic groups with very strong ancestral ties, are most likely to report contact with the dead.[10]

**Table 8.6: Number of Different Kinds of Psychic or Mystical Experience Reported by Those Who Have at Least One of the Five Experiences Frequently**

| Number of Different Kinds of Experience | Percentage of Those Who Report One of Five Experiences Frequently |
|---|---|
| 1 | 75 |
| 2 | 20 |
| 3 | 4 |
| 4 | 1 |
| 5 | 1 |
| Total | 101 |
| N = | (263)[a] |

a. Eighteen percent of total sample.

Rather surprisingly, there is not much overlap in the kinds of psychic or mystical experience reported by those who have such experiences frequently (Table 8.6). Three-quarters of those who report frequent experiences have had them in only one of our five categories, and only a handful of our respondents have had them in more than two. Detailed examination of the various kinds of psychic experiences will have to wait for the monograph which will come from this research. It is sufficient to note at the present time these various types of experiences. However—and we trust that this is a point our colleagues in the research profession will not miss—eighteen percent of our representative national sample have had at least one of the varieties of psychic or mystical experiences *frequently.* That means there are thirty-six million Americans who frequently undergo some kind of paranormal interlude. It is a phenomenon that can hardly be ignored any longer.

## Mystical Experiences in Contemporary Society

We intend, in this chapter, to explore the relationship between ultimate values and mystical experiences. In some of the previous research on mystical experiences, authors have noted that many people may have such experiences, but they may be lacking in the language with which to give their experience expression. It is certainly plausible, then, that people with a world view compatible with the existence of a benevolent spiritual force would be more likely to express interaction with such a force than those with a malevolent view of ultimate reality.

We will explore the hypothesis that ultimate values act as a link between childhood religious atmosphere and adult ecstatic interludes. The atmosphere sensitizes the individual to the religious component of life and predisposes one to a certain set of ultimate values which then permits the individual to experience ecstasy, as we have delineated it, and also to communicate that experience to others. We note in Table 8.7 that there is indeed a relationship between one's position in the ultimate values typology and having ecstatic experiences. Almost half of the hopefuls (forty-nine percent) have had such an experience at least once, while slightly fewer of the religious optimists (forty-two percent)

Table 8.7: Mystical Experience by Ultimate Values (in percentages)

| Values | Never | Once or twice | Several times | Frequently | Total |
|---|---|---|---|---|---|
| Religious optimist | 58 | 16 | 19 | 7 | 100 |
| Hopeful | 51 | 20 | 19 | 10 | 100 |
| Secular optimist | 68 | 19 | 9 | 4 | 100 |
| Pessimist | 72 | 18 | 9 | 21 | 100 |
| Diffuse | 70 | 21 | 6 | 3 | 100 |

report the same. In the three remaining types, the proportion reporting ecstatic interludes falls to approximately thirty percent.

We will investigate in some detail here the variables that relate to mystical experience, and then attempt to build a causal model to "explain" that experience. This model-building will illustrate techniques that we will use in further analysis of all the material presented in this preliminary report.

An inspection of preliminary cross-tabulations revealed, as we expected, that the most interesting patterns of association occurred for those who have frequent ecstatic experiences. Unfortunately, since they are only five percent of the total population, correlation and regression analysis (currently the most popular form of causal modeling) was impossible. We therefore turned to two-by-two contingency tables, an analytic technique which has undergone a notable rehabilitation recently through the work of Goodman and Davis.[11] In the tables that follow, virtually all q's over .3 are significant at the .001 level, and q's over .2 are significant at the .01 level. In addition, some of the q's over .15 are significant at the .05 level. For the most part, we shall limit ourselves to q's in excess of .2 in this commentary.

If mystics came from socially oppressed groups, one would expect them to be disproportionately young, female, black, and lower-income. In fact, however, mystics are more likely to be over forty, male, college-educated, and making over $10,000 a year (Table 8.8). They are, however, substantially more likely to be black (.52) and Protestant(.53).

Those who think of mystics as being unhappy, maladjusted people who seek relief would also predict that mystics come from rigid, harsh, and inflexible families. Our own assumptions, based on the theoretical perspective we derived from the work of Luck-

**Table 8.8: Measures of Association Between Frequent Experiences of Mystical Ecstasy and Demographic Variables (Yule's Q)**

| | |
|---|---|
| Age (over 40) | .35 |
| Sex (female) | −.19 |
| Race (black) | .52 |
| Religion (Protestant) | .53 |
| Education (college) | .33 |
| Income (over $10,000) | .18 |

mann and Geertz, and from McCready's research, led us to expect a background of warm family relationships and a joyous approach to religion. Table 8.9 seems to support our approach. While there was no association between ecstasy and closeness between parents (much to our surprise), there were strong associations with closeness between the respondent and parents, with the mother's church attendance, and with the joyousness of both parents' religious approach (at least as the respondent remembered that approach). McCready's research has indicated that as far as transmission of religious behavior is concerned, the father is considerably more important than the mother. However, Table 8.9 suggests that, for ecstasy in adult life, the mother may well be more important than the father. In any case, growing up in a supportive and religiously joyous family atmosphere turns out to be conducive to frequent mystical experiences.

A religiously joyous and supportive family atmosphere is also conducive to a general satisfaction with one's life (Table 8.10). As a child, mystics were not notably above the average in life satisfactions, but in the teen years, "now," and for expectations of "five years from now," they are substantially above the average. Furthermore, while they do not remember their childhood to be

**Table 8.9: Measures of Association Between Frequent Experiences of Mystical Ecstasy and Family Experience (Yule's Q)**

| | |
|---|---|
| Closeness between mother and father | .04 |
| Closeness between respondent and mother | .29 |
| Closeness between respondent and father | .19 |
| Mother's church attendance (almost every week or more) | .00 |
| Father's church attendance (almost every week or more) | .44 |
| Joyousness of father's religion | .36 |
| Joyousness of mother's religion | .43 |

**Table 8.10: Measures of Association Between Frequent Mystical Ecstasy and Life Satisfaction Ladder[a] (Yule's Q)**

| | |
|---|---|
| Child | .15 |
| Teen | .32 |
| Now | .31 |
| Five years from now | .33 |

a. A ten-point scale between "the best your life could be" and "the worst your life could be."

more religious than do other respondents, their adolescence, their present and future religious situations (Table 8.11) are described as substantially more religious than those of the rest of the population. The fact that both satisfaction and religious behavior seem to move notably above the average in their adolescent years suggests the possibility that mystical experiences may have begun then, or perhaps may have been more self-consciously perceived at that time.[12] Much of the autobiographical literature of mystics does indeed begin with a description of an adolescent experience.[13]

Our data scarcely suggest repressed, unhappy, rigid, guilt-ridden, puzzled people. It could well be, of course, that the conflicts are deeply repressed in their personalities. It is also difficult to say whether the mystical experience induced life satisfaction or whether a higher level of life satisfaction created a personality open to mystical experience. But our data at least raise the possibility that mysticism may well be good for you. Surely the findings presented in Table 8.12 would confirm such a hunch. There is a correlation of .34 between mystical experience and positive affect on the Bradburn psychological well-being scale, and a correlation of .31 on a negative affect scale (which means that mystics are low on negative affect).[14] The result of this combination is a whopping .4 association between mystical experience and balance affect or "happiness." While their marriages are no better or no

**Table 8.11: Measures of Association Between Mystical Ecstasy and Religious Ladder[a] (Yule's Q)**

| | |
|---|---|
| Child | .16 |
| Teen | .47 |
| Now | .68 |
| Five years from now | .73 |

a. "Most religious you could be" versus "The least religious you could be."

**Table 8.12: Measures of Association Between Frequent Mystical Ecstasy and Psychological Well-Being[a] (Yule's Q)**

| | |
|---|---|
| Positive affect | .34 |
| Negative affect | −.31 |
| Balance affect | .40 |
| Positive marriage | .09 |
| Negative marriage | .04 |
| Marriage balance | .05 |

a. Bradburn "happiness scales."

worse than the rest of the population, the frequent mystic reports a state of psychological well-being substantially higher than the national average. We would suggest that this is a finding of considerable importance and merits much further research.

White mystics (Table 8.13) are also substantially less likely to be racist than the national population. Whether mystical interludes "cause" their racial enlightenment or whether tolerance and openness to mystical experience are both related to antecedent cultural and psychological factors is difficult to say on the basis of a one-shot survey. But whatever the flow of causality, the negative correlation between ecstasy and racism seems to be one more nail in the coffin of the theory that ecstatics are rigid, haunted, unhappy people.

We would also expect that if the indicators of ultimate values we have devised do indeed get at fundamental orientations toward the cosmos, there would be a relationship between these values and mystical experience. We have already seen that the hopefuls and the religious optimists are more likely to have such experiences than the other types (Table 8.7), but we would like to examine that relationship from a slightly different perspective here. More specifically, we would expect that these respondents who are high on the religious optimism and hopefulness attitude scales, as well as the religious optimists and the hopefuls from the typology,

**Table 8.13: Measures of Association Between Frequent Mystical Ecstasy and Certain Attitudes and Values (Yule's Q)**

| | |
|---|---|
| Racism | −.27 |
| Conservative authoritarianism | −.09 |
| Liberal authoritarianism | −.13 |

would also be more likely to have mystical experiences. We would also expect that those with high indicators of hopefulness would be most likely of all to have such experiences, since their approach to religion suggests more depth than the facile approach of the optimists.

The data in Table 8.14 support these assumptions. The coefficient between the hopeful attitude measure and mysticism is .72 and the coefficient for the hopefuls from the typology is .42. Both the attitude items and the vignettes operate in the same direction, which adds to the argument that our measures of ultimate values are valid indicators. Religious optimism as measured by both methods is the next most closely associated perspective to mysticism, the secular measures tend to be in the middle, and the indicators of pessimism are strongly associated with *not* having had ecstatic interludes (or at least with not having reported them).

We would be hard put to say with certainty which way the causality runs in these relationships. Are hopeful people more likely to be open to ecstatic experiences, or are those who have had such experiences more likely to be hopeful as a result? Our own guess is that the childhood religious environment produces a hopeful religious orientation, which in turn permits an openness and receptivity toward mystical experiences. These experiences, then, deepen and strengthen the conviction of hopefulness in a cycle of reinforcement.

We might add in passing that the relationships reported in Table 8.14 provide some validation for the basic belief system measures.

Table 8.14: Measures of Association Between Frequent Mystical Ecstasy and Basic Belief Systems (Yule's Q)

| | |
|---|---|
| *Opinion Scales* | |
| Religious optimism | 40 |
| Agnosticism | −.31 |
| Secular optimism | .05 |
| Hopefulness | .72 |
| | |
| *Vignette Scales* | |
| Religious optimism | .27 |
| Hopefulness | .42 |
| Secular optimism | −.18 |
| Pessimism | −.62 |
| Diffuse | −.18 |

We might well expect that basic belief scales, if they had any use at all, would indeed differentiate on mystics who are in one respect "religiously sensitive" individuals.

We noted previously that the ecstatics in our research were disproportionately black. Is the pattern of relationships between ecstasy and other variables different for them than for whites (Table 8.15)? The association between college attendance and ecstasy is even higher for blacks than for whites, though, surprisingly enough, there is a negative association for black ecstatics and being Protestant. It is also very clear that there are substantial differences in childhood experiences for the black mystics. Among the white mystics, there is an association between mystical experience and closeness between parents, which we had hypothesized for the entire sample. But this relationship is −.7 for blacks. On the other hand, the association between respondent-mother relationship and mysticism disappears for whites and becomes .58 for blacks.

Finally, joyousness in parental religion was an important variable in the background of white mystics. When the racial control was introduced, the father's joyousness became slightly more important than the mother's. But the mother's joyousness is unimportant in the background of black mystics, and the father's joyousness is negatively related. Nor do blacks manifest high life

Table 8.15: Measures of Association Between Frequent Mystical Ecstasy and Other Variables by Race (Yule's Q)

|  | White | Black |
| --- | --- | --- |
| Education | .33 | .47 |
| Religion | .64 | −.20 |
| Closeness of parents | .27 | −.57 |
| Closeness of respondent to mother | −.20 | .58 |
| Closeness of respondent to father | . . . | . . . |
| Joyousness of father's religion | .47 | −.24 |
| Joyousness of mother's religion | .43 | .09 |
| Life Satisfaction |  |  |
| Child | .16 | .05 |
| Teen | .35 | .10 |
| Now | .30 | .33 |
| Five years from now | .36 | .04 |
| Balance affect | .40 | .46 |
| Racism | −.27 | . . . |

satisfactions in the teen years or expect high satisfactions for the future. The association between mystical experience and life satisfaction now is virtually the same for the two groups, but the blacks do not project that satisfaction backward into the past or forward into the future. However, no matter what their past memories are or their expectations for the future, the association between the Bradburn balance affect scale and mysticism for blacks is even higher than it is for whites.

There are clearly very different patterns of mystical experiences for the two racial groups. Indeed, a number of the hypotheses that we had expected to be confirmed for the whole population were in fact sustained only for whites. They were so strongly rejected among the blacks that when the two groups were considered together, the expected correlations were not observable. Black mysticism relates neither to happy youth nor expectations for a happy future, but it does relate very powerfully to a close relationship with one's mother. It also, surprisingly enough, relates to higher education and to not being Protestant. Therefore, our black mystics are not disproportionately poor members of fundamentalist congregations, as might have been expected. Much further research with larger samples is clearly required.[15]

There is probably no way of wording a question about a mystical experience that will be perfectly satisfactory—surely not one that could be administered in a national survey. There are, one supposes, some people who get profoundly shook up emotionally when a forty-eight-year-old George Blanda puts the ball between the uprights for the ten thousandth time, or when Henry Aaron knocks the baseball over the centerfield for the seven hundred fifteenth time. We therefore try to determine two things: What "triggered" the experience, and how people would describe their experience. Table 8.16 presents the rank order of triggers (for all those who had at least one mystical experience). The beauties of nature, moments of quiet reflection, church services, and sermons were all mentioned by two-fifths of those who had such experiences. Interestingly enough, none of our sample reported that the experience was drug-induced, suggesting at least the possibility that mysticism need not rely on hallucinogenic drugs at all.

We had expected that a factor analysis would produce a religious and an esthetic factor. As we discovered in Table 8.17, our

Table 8.16: Triggers of Mystical Experiences

| Triggers | Percentage |
| --- | --- |
| Listening to music | 49 |
| Prayer | 48 |
| Beauties of nature such as sunset | 45 |
| Moments of quiet reflection | 42 |
| Attending church service | 41 |
| Listening to sermon | 40 |
| Watching little children | 34 |
| Reading the bible | 34 |
| Being alone in church | 30 |
| Reading a poem or a novel | 21 |
| Childbirth | 20 |
| Sexual love-making | 18 |
| Your own creative work | 17 |
| Looking at a painting | 15 |
| Something else | 13 |
| Physical exercise | 1 |
| Drugs | 0 |

expectations were correct. In addition, a third factor emerged loading heavily on childbirth and sexual love-making.

Among the descriptions of mystical experience (Table 8.18), feelings of peace, a certainty that all things work out, a sense of need to contribute to others, a conviction that love is the center of everything, and a sense of joy and laughter were mentioned by more than two-fifths of those who had had such experiences—a

Table 8.17: Mystical Trigger Factors (factor loadings)

| Triggers | Aesthetic | Religious | Sexual |
| --- | --- | --- | --- |
| Listening to music | −.56 | ... | ... |
| Prayer | ... | .62 | ... |
| Beauties of nature | −.47 | ... | ... |
| Moments of quiet reflection | −.40 | ... | ... |
| Attending church service | ... | .53 | ... |
| Listening to sermon | ... | .63 | ... |
| Watching little children | −.33 | ... | ... |
| Reading the bible | ... | .64 | ... |
| Being alone in church | −.25 | ... | ... |
| Reading a poem or a novel | −.64 | ... | ... |
| Childbirth | ... | ... | −.53 |
| Sexual love-making | ... | ... | −.33 |
| Your own creative work | −.54 | ... | ... |
| Looking at a painting | −.58 | ... | ... |

## Table 8.18: "Descriptors" of Mystical Experience

|  | Percentage |
| --- | --- |
| A feeling of deep and profound peace | 55 |
| A certainty that all things would work out for the good | 48 |
| Sense of my own need to contribute to others  *! ← social/synergy* | 43 |
| A conviction that love is at the center of everything  *⌣* | 43 |
| Sense of joy and laughter | 43 |
| An experience of great emotional intensity | 38 |
| A great increase in my understanding and knowledge | 32 |
| A sense of the unity of everything and my own part in it  *(cosmic cons.)* | 29 |
| A sense of a new life or living in a new world  *(re-born)* | 27 |
| A confidence in my own personal survival | 27 |
| A feeling that I couldn't possibly describe what was happening to me  *(ineffable)* | 26 |
| The sense that all the universe is alive | 25 |
| The sensation that my personality has been taken over by something much more powerful than I am | 24 |
| A sense of tremendous personal expansion, either psychological or physical | 22 |
| A sensation of warmth or fire | 22 |
| A sense of being alone | 19 |
| A loss of concern about worldly problems | 19 |
| A sense that I was being bathed in light | 14 |
| A feeling of desolation  *?* | 8 |
| Something else | 4 |

finding in keeping with Maslow's description of core religious experience, as well as many of the autobiographical accounts of mystics themselves. It is interesting to note that one-fifth of the respondents reported a sense of being alone, and eight percent a feeling of desolation (which are aspects of ecstasy that escaped both Maslow and the counter culture enthusiasts, although they never escaped such masters of the mystical tradition as John of the Cross, who was all too painfully aware of the "dark night of the soul" phenomenon).

We were much less confident of what sort of factors would emerge from factor analysis of the description items. We guessed that there might be one factor that would describe internal emotions—knowledge, peace, joy, etc.—and another that might describe more the phenomenon of being "taken over" by some powerful outside force. To some extent, this expectation was confirmed by the descriptions in Table 8.19. The first factor, which we call "hot" mysticism, heavily loads on feelings of intensity, unity, knowledge, peace, life, and joy—though it also includes the "dark night" item. Factor two, which we call "cool," loads heavily on the ineffability, rebirth, being taken over, and being bathed in light aspects of the experience. Two other factors emerged, one emphasizing that love is the center of the universe, certainty of survival, confidence that things would work out for the good, and the need to make a contribution to others. It seemed to us that this represented a "harmony in the universe" factor. The last factor is composed of merely one item, the confidence in survival.

Table 8.19: Factors for Mystical "Descriptor" Items (factor loadings)

| Descriptors | Hot | Cool | Harmony | Survival |
|---|---|---|---|---|
| Sense of new life or living in a new world | ... | .38 | ... | ... |
| Sense of unity and my own part in it | −.54 | ... | ... | ... |
| An experience of great emotional intensity | −.61 | ... | ... | ... |
| Great increase in understanding and knowledge | −.30 | ... | ... | ... |
| Feeling of deep and profound peace | −.29 | ... | ... | ... |
| Sense of joy and laughter | −.56 | ... | ... | ... |
| Sense of need to contribute to others | ... | ... | −.52 | ... |
| Sensation of warmth or fire | −.44 | ... | ... | ... |
| Sense of being bathed in light | ... | .55 | ... | ... |
| Couldn't possibly describe what was happening | ... | .38 | ... | ... |
| Sensation that personality was taken over by something more powerful than I | ... | .63 | ... | ... |
| Sense of being alone | −.38 | ... | ... | ... |
| Certainty that all things work out for the good | ... | ... | −.54 | ... |
| Confidence in personal survival | ... | ... | −.44 | .56 |
| Sense of personal expansion, either psychological or physical | −.40 | ... | ... | ... |
| Conviction that love is at the center of everything | ... | ... | −.52 | ... |
| A sense that all the universe is alive | −.34 | ... | ... | ... |

## Mystical Experiences and Ultimate Values

Thus far in this chapter, we have strayed away from the basic belief typology that provided the framework for much of the rest of this report. Now that we have developed all the major variables from our ecstatic experience questions, it is appropriate to ask whether there is any difference among the ultimate value groups in the frequency and style of their mystical experiences. We would be in some trouble if there were such differences, because a set of ultimate values that had no relationship with such an intense and "ultimate" experience as mystical ecstasy would fall under immediate suspicion.

However, as we see in Table 8.20, there are very considerable differences. More than two-fifths of the religious optimists and nearly one-half of the hopefuls report such experiences, while less than one-third of the pessimists or the diffused have had ecstatic episodes. The first two groups are also more likely to have experiences frequently—eight percent of the religious optimists and eleven percent of the hopefuls.

Since the more frequent the experience, the more likely the reporting of multiple triggers and descriptors, it is not surprising that many of the signs of the standardized scores in the last three

**Table 8.20: Mystical Experiences by Value Types**

| Item | Religious Optimist | Hopeful | Secular Optimist | Pessimist | Diffuse |
|---|---|---|---|---|---|
| *Percentage* | | | | | |
| Ever | 42 | 42 | 32 | 28 | 30 |
| Frequent | 8 | 10 | 4 | 2 | 3 |
| N = | (308) | (317) | (204) | (328) | (247) |
| | | | | | |
| *Standard Points (factor scales)* | | | | | |
| Aesthetic trigger | −13 | 11 | 05 | 02 | −09 |
| Religious trigger | 18 | 22 | −06 | −33 | −32 |
| Sexual trigger | −04 | 06 | 02 | 00 | −08 |
| Hot mystic descriptor | −09 | 08 | 00 | −05 | 03 |
| Cool mystic descriptor | 12 | 11 | 02 | −18 | −21 |
| Harmony descriptor | 10 | 13 | 06 | −29 | −16 |
| Survival descriptor | 01 | 06 | 03 | −12 | −04 |
| N = | (130) | (156) | (65) | (92) | (74) |

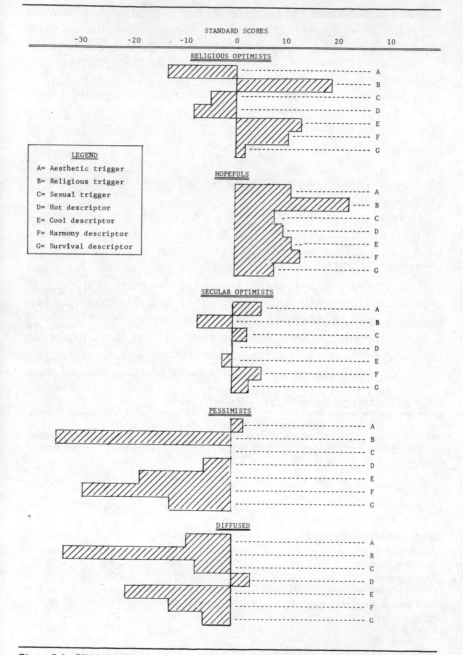

Figure 8.1: STANDARD SCORES ON THE TRIGGER AND DESCRIPTION FACTORS BY ULTIMATE VALUE TYPES

columns are minuses. The critical issue is the difference between the religious optimists and thefuls. About two-fifths of both groups report having had such experiences. Differences between them on the trigger and descriptor scales would indicate that ultimate values do indeed shape one's experience of the ultimate in intense mystical episodes.

The pattern of relationships that emerges from the bottom part of Table 8.20 is a fascinating one, which we present graphically in Figure 8.1. Most interesting, for our purposes, is the differentiation between the religious optimists and the hopefuls. The two patterns are similar, with the exception of the aesthetic trigger, the sexual trigger, and the "hot" mysticism descriptor. The hopefuls are more likely than the religious optimists to have their ecstatic episodes triggered by aesthetic or sexual experiences, and to have the "hot," as opposed to the "cool," type of mystical interlude. Both are likely to report religious triggers, and the hopeful are slightly more likely to report having had "harmony" and "survival" experiences. (The "survival" experiences being discussed here are measured by an entirely different item than that used for the measure discussed in Table 5.7.) Thus, the relationship between hopefulness and the expectation of survival is confirmed by two different measures, as well as being related to an experience of some contact with "ultimate reality."

It would appear that those with a world view of "religious optimism" have religious experiences which are "proper" and "dignified," while those with a "hopeful" perspective have experiences which are wider, wilder, and more passionate. The hopefuls are emerging in this study as balanced and judicious human beings. They acknowledge the existence and the power of evil and the slifhtly superior power of good in the universe. They are more likely to trust other people, they are tolerant of racial differences, and they steer a careful middle course on most issues. But they are more likely to think of themselves as close to God, more likely to believe in their own survival, and now, it turns out, they are capable of fiery religious experiences. And they are more likely to report sexually triggered experiences than any of the other types.

The secular optimists are very close to the mean for all of the triggers and descriptors, as we would expect. The pessimists and the diffused are well below the mean on most of the trigger and descriptor factors, which is also what one would expect given their attitude toward the religious element of life as documented in Chapter 5.

## Models for Mysticism

We conclude this chapter with an exploratory causal analysis that utilizes the log linear techniques developed by Goodman, Davis, and others.[16]

We have assumed that a mystical interlude is a cognitive experience (because that is what those who have them say they are). We have further assumed that it is a religious experience in the Geertzian sense of dealing with an ultimate world view. It therefore seems reasonable to assume that those factors which influence the development of basic world views will also relate to the experience of ecstasy. It is also not unreasonable to assume that the "ordinary" basic belief system which suffices for the nonecstatic segments of life will predispose one to mystical interludes (or not predispose, depending on the world view of the respondent). Finally, it may be not unreasonable to assume that the basic belief system *mediates* between factors which shape it, and the ecstatic episode, also shaped by the same factors.

For our causal model we set out the following hypotheses:

(1) Mystical experiences will relate to the family structure and culture which the person experiences when he or she was growing up.

(2) Closeness to parents during adolescence will predict mystical experience.

(3) Religiousness of parents will predict mystical experience.

(4) The joyousness of parental religious style will predict mystical experience.

(5) Closeness to father, father's joy, and father's religiousness will all be more important than mother's.

(6) The effect of these adolescent experiences will be mediated by the basic belief system of the individual. Father's joyousness, for example, will lead to greater hopefulness, which in turn will increase the likelihood of ecstasy.

Table 8.21: A Typology of Mystics—For All Who Have at Least One Mystical Experience (in percentages)

| | |
|---|---|
| Super mystics—high on hot, cool, and harmony | 20 |
| Cool mystics—high on cool, low on others | 6 |
| Hot mystics—high on hot, low on others | 7 |
| Harmony mystics—high on harmony, low on others | 10 |
| Hot-cool mystics—high on hot, high on cool, low on harmony | 4 |
| Hot harmony mystics—high on hot, high on harmony, low on cool | 8 |
| Cool harmony mystics—high on cool, high on harmony, low on hot | 7 |
| Quiet mystics—low on all three | 37 |

Since we have only seventy-five frequent mystics in our sample, the usual multiple regression-path analytic approach to causal analysis could be used. We needed a technique that is relatively independent of marginal distribution. Fortunately, the log linear method developed by Goodman does not depend on marginal, since it uses logs rather than numbers. More fortunately, the *Social Indicators* team at NORC has developed a conversational program for using Goodman's techniques, and most fortunately of all, they were willing and patient enough to give us a crash course in using the system.[1][7]

Briefly, we had that rare experience in social research of seeing almost all of our expectations sustained. Closeness to father, joyousness of father's religious style, and father's church attendance all do predict frequent mystical experience (see Figure 8.2). The relationship between closeness to mother and ecstasy is not significant when closeness to father is taken into account. Nor does the relationship to mother survive a significance test. (In Table 8.9, we established that there was no relationship between the mother's church attendance and ecstasy.) Furthermore, in a model using both closeness to father and father's joy, it is clear that the father's joy is of decisive importance. Finally, when father's church attendance and father's joy are put into the same model, both are significant, although father's joy is the more important of the two. (We may note here that the log linear approach still lacks an equivalent of R, the multiple regression statistic.)

In Figure 8.3, we note that the same models seem to work for both sexes, with father's church attendance being important for males, and closeness to mother having some impact on men—the

a. Frequent mystical experiences by closeness to mother and to father.

b. Frequent mystical experiences by joyousness of father's approach to religion and joyousness of mother's approach to religion.

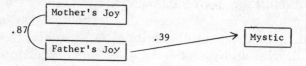

c. Frequent mystical experience by closeness to father and joyousness of father's approach to religion.

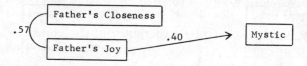

d. Frequent mystical experience by joyousness of father's approach to religion and father's church attendance.

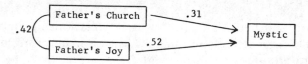

*For all models, given the null hypothesis that the described effect is absent has been rejected at significant levels. All normed parameters given are also significant.

Figure 8.2: LOG LINEAR MODELS* FOR MYSTICISM AND FAMILY BACKGROUND VARIABLES

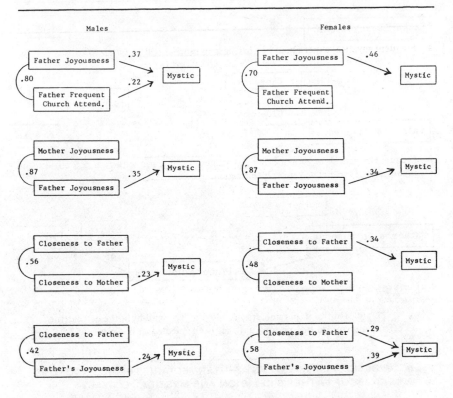

*The null hypotheses that the effects shown are not present have all been rejected at a significant level.

Figure 8.3: RELATIONSHIPS BETWEEN FAMILY STRUCTURE AND FREQUENT MYSTICAL EXPERIENCE BY SEX*

only place in our analysis where the relationship to mother becomes important.

So, childhood experiences, particularly of a religiously joyous father, are predictors of frequent mystical experiences in adult life. Are these childhood experiences mediated by the basic belief systems that McCready's research addressed? It is clear from Figure 8.4 that they seem to be. Hopefulness, religious optimism, and agnosticism all serve as links between the joyousness of fathers and frequent experience of ecstasy in adult life. In each case, the direct relationship between the childhood and adult experiences is not significant, while the two legs of the indirect relationship

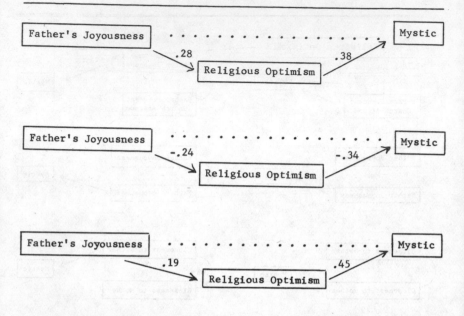

*Only significant parameters are shown. The null-hypotheses that the effects shown are not present have all been rejected at a significant level.

Figure 8.4: BASIC BELIEF SYSTEMS AS INTERMEDIARIES BETWEEN JOYOUS-NESS OF FATHER'S RELIGION AND MYSTICAL ECSTASY*

(through basic belief) are. The causal lines could, of course, be reversed. It may well be that frequent mysticism interludes mediate between paternal religious joy and belief. We think that the prior link is more probable, since we have some theoretical and empirical reason for believing that the basic belief system (or interpretive scheme) is formed very early in life and is not subject to substantial modification in subsequent years. However, until longitudinal research is undertaken, one pays one's money and takes one's choice. Fortunately, we have a sample of the adolescent children of the members of our original sample and will be able to explore the question of the transmission of basic belief systems, as well as the transmission of mystical propensities across generational lines.

Finally, in Figure 8.5 we try to construct a model of the relationship between basic belief systems and ecstasy. In the final

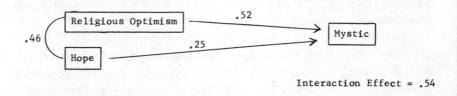

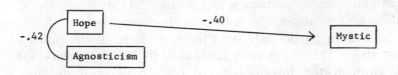

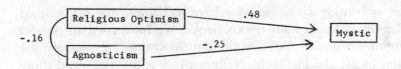

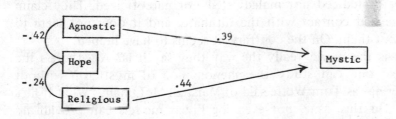

*All parameters are significant, all models represent rejected null hypotheses.

Figure 8.5: BASIC BELIEF SYSTEMS AND ECSTASY*

model at the bottom of the page we note that agnosticism has an indirect (and negative) relationship through hopefulness with frequent ecstasy, while hopefulness and religious optimism have substantial, positive, and relatively equal relationships with ecstasy. (It should be noted, by the way, that the first time you manage to fit a four-variable model may not exactly be an ecstatic experience in our sense of the term, but it is a hell of a lot of fun. Our instructors are experimenting with a six-variable model, which is mind-boggling.)

In summary, mysticism seems to result in part from childhood and adolescent relationships with parents, particularly with the father, and more particularly with the joyousness of the father's religious style. This joyousness leads to a higher propensity for ecstasy through the intermediary of basic belief systems, particularly of hopefulness and religious optimism. There may be a certain madness—or at least unmitigated gall—in using survey instruments, computer analysis, and log linear models to deal with what is, according to those who have had them, the ultimate, if not The Ultimate, in human experience. We have tried to ponder the imponderable, to measure the unmeasurable, to quantify the absolute, to eff the ineffable. Neither of us is mystical, and those we know who are, find our efforts diverting, but hardly profound. Still, what survey research can do, it will do. There are a lot of mystics around, more than anyone ever thought existed. They are neither prejudiced nor maladjusted nor narcoticized. They claim to have had contact with the ultimate, and it does not seem to have hurt them. On the contrary, it seems to have helped.

But is the world really the way they say it is? Ah, there's the rub. No one can study the phenomenon of mysticism without wondering, as Tom Wolfe said of Marshall McLuhan, "What if he's right? On this issue, not even log linear models can provide an answer. Let us then end this discussion where we began. Professor William James said, "Non-mystics are under no obligation to acknowledge in mystical states a superior authority conferred on them by their intrinsic nature. Yet . . . the existence of mystical states absolutely overthrows the pretension of nonmystical states to be the sole and ultimate dictator of what we may believe."

Beyond that uneasy agnoticism, social science cannot go.

# NOTES

1. The parapsychologists, some of the worlds' most serious people, have recently protested about the appropriation of their discipline by the counter culture.

2. For a collection of articles from this perspective, see *The Highest States of Consciousness*, edited by John White, New York: Doubleday, 1972.

3. Abraham Maslow, ibid.

4. Linda B. Bourque, "Social Correlates of Transcendental Experience," *Sociological Analysis*, Vol. 20, Fall 1969, pp. 151-163. ――― and Kurt Back, "Values in Transcendental Experiences," *Social Forces*, Vol. 47, September 1970, pp. 34-38. ――― "Language, Society and Subjective Experience," *Sociometry*, Vol. 34, 1971, pp. 1-21.

5. Marganita Laski, *Ecstasy: The Study of Some Secular and Religious Experiences*, Westport, Conn.: Greenwood Press, 1968.

6. Phillip Ennis, "Ecstasy and Everyday Life," *Journal for the Scientific Study of Religion*, Vol. 6, 1967, pp. 40-49.

7. Thomas Luckmann, *The Invisible Religion*, New York: Macmillan, 1967. Clifford Geertz, *The Interpretation of Cultures*, New York: Basic Books, 1973, pp. 87-141.

8. There is theoretical justification for this assumption in the work of Geertz and Luckmann, and empirical validation in the work of McCready.

9. Personal recollections of a seminar conversation with Clifford Geertz at the National Opinion Research Center during the Spring of 1972.

10. Having made the discovery that more than half the Irish Protestants in our sample reported having at least one ecstatic interlude, we promptly interviewed two Scots-Irish social scientists of our acquaintance. One evaded the question, and the other admitted off the record that he had had two such experiences. We will keep a very careful eye on the corridors of the NORC building in the future.

11. Leo Goodman, "The Analysis of Multidimensional Contingency Tables When Some Variables Are Posterior to Others: A Modified Path Analysis Approach," *Biometrika*, Vol. 60, 1973, pp. 179-192. James A. Davis, "Survey Replications, Log Linear Models, and Theories of Social Change," NORC, lithographed, 1973.

12. One mystic we interviewed in person could not recall a time in life when such experiences were not occurring.

13. F. C. Happhold, *Mysticism: A Study and Anthology*, Middlesex, Eng.: Penguin, 1964.

14. Norman Bradburn, op. cit.

15. In Table 8.15, we have left out all the items on which blacks and whites are similar. There were very small differences between the two groups in the size of the measures of association for such things as sex, age, and ultimate values.

16. James A. Davis, op. cit.

17. The interactive program is named CATFIT3.

*Chapter 9*

## VALUE-ORIENTED EDUCATION AND

## ULTIMATE VALUES

One of the perennial debates in American society is whether values can be taught in school. Much of the current research on the impact of education suggests not only that values cannot be taught, but that very little else is taught either. Schools, it seems, can pass on certain skills and information (though the reception of such skills is conditioned by the student's social class background), but values, motivations, and the desire to achieve in an achievement-oriented society are susceptible of transmission in the classroom environment.

Some of those who have reviewed the literature on the lack of success of value-education cite the 1963 NORC study, *The Education of Catholic Americans,* as one of the first research enterprises that pointed to the failure of schools as the purveyors of values. Catholic schools, such commentators argue, are unable to transmit values; and if they can't, who can? (See, for example, the introduction to the collected essays of Daniel P. Moynihan, *Coping.*)[1] The findings of *The Education of Catholic Americans* are not easily summarized. Under some circumstances and on some sorts of values, parochial schools had relatively little impact, and under other circumstances, with regard to other values, they had a modest and occasionally substantial impact. For example, those who had received all their grammar school, high school, and college education in Catholic schools were substantially lower on measures of racism and anti-Semitism than other Catholics and the American population in general. Furthermore, parochial school Catholics were more likely to engage in religious devotional practices than their public school counterparts.[2] Far from this difference being explained by variations in family religious practices, the difference is most notable between parochial school Catholics and the public school Catholics who came from families with strong devotional practices. Within the Catholic community there were two principal reactions to these findings:

(1) Among those supporters of parochial schools who did not think the differences were big enough to justify the schools, it was said, "Church attendance is not the same thing as religion."

(2) Among those proponents of parochial schools who were not prepared to believe the possibility of the modest differences discovered by *The Education of Catholic Americans,* it was said, "Church attendance is not the same thing as religion."

The point made by both the critics and the proponents of parochial education is valid enough, but, given the heavy emphasis on frequent church attendance as a symbol of religious loyalty in American Catholicism, it was not a bad measure to use. The present project enables us, however, to turn to something more basic and fundamental than church attendance—the respondent's conception of the nature of reality as it actually is.

But the question is of onterest not merely as a means of pouring fuel on the fire of the perennial parochial school debate. We have already established in this report that family relationships and family religious practice have an effect on the basic belief systems of American adults. Are the ultimate values susceptible of modification or development by any other institution of socialization? One would be inclined to suspect that if a parochial school, designed explicitly and consciously to reinforce the transmission of certain religious values, does not have an impact on religious socialization, then most other institutions would surely not do so.

*Parochial Schools, Hopefulness, and*
*Psychological Well-Being*

It seems to us to be safe to assume that the Catholic parochial schools would be interested in transmitting and reinforcing the value system that we have called "hopeful." Our own (we suspect not heretical) understanding of the Christian tradition is that the hopeful ultimate value system is the best statement of the Christian world view. (Though heaven knows we both have heard in our collective thirty-two years in Catholic schools statements of world views that were anything but hopeful.)

The critical question, then, is whether those who have attended Catholic schools are more likely to fall into the "hopeful" category of our religious typology. Somewhat to our surprise, Catholic-school Catholics are indeed more likely to be found among the hopeful; in fact, twenty-nine percent of those who attended Catholic grammar schools and high schools are hopefuls, as opposed to seventeen percent of those who did not attend Catholic school at all. Those who had some of their education in Catholic schools are in between. If the data reported in Table 9.1 can stand up in the face of further analysis, then it would appear that a strong case can be made that religious schools are successful in transmitting and reinforcing basic values. (One would have to know first, of course, whether parents with hopeful world views are more likely to send their children to parochial schools than were other parents. This is a question which can be addressed to some extent in the cross-generational analysis, to appear in a later monograph, based on a present project, and in a replication of the education of Catholic Americans currently under way at NORC.)

We do know from *The Education of Catholic Americans* that those who had all their education in parochial schools are more likely to have a higher level of educational attainment (mostly because they come from more economically advantaged families). Therefore we must consider the possibility that their higher scores on hopefulness are merely the effect of greater educational attainment.

The evidence presented in Table 9.2 suggests that such is not the case. The differences among the three groups in the percentage of hopefuls diminish sharply among those who did not go to

**Table 9.1: Ultimate Value Typology for Catholics by Parochial School Attendance (in percentages)**

| Ultimate Value Type | Catholic Grammar and High School | Either Grammar or High School | Neither |
|---|---|---|---|
| Religious optimist | 18 | 21 | 21 |
| Hopeful | 29 | 23 | 17 |
| Secular optimist | 12 | 6 | 13 |
| Pessimist | 24 | 33 | 26 |
| Diffuse | 17 | 17 | 24 |
| Total | 100 | 100 | 100 |
| N = | (97) | (104) | (147) |

college; but it is precisely among the college-educated that the greatest differences are to be found, with thirty percent of those who attended both Catholic grammar school and Catholic high school being hopeful as opposed to sixteen percent of those with no Catholic schooling. It is precisely among the better-educated that the impact of parochial school religious socialization seems to have been the greatest.

**Table 9.2: Ultimate Value Typology for Catholics by Parochial School Attendance by Level of Education (in percentages)**

| Ultimate Value Type | Catholic Grammar, High School | Either | Neither |
|---|---|---|---|
| *High School Graduate or Less* | | | |
| Religious optimist | 25 | 19 | 24 |
| Hopeful | 28 | 24 | 17 |
| Secular optimist | 10 | 8 | 12 |
| Pessimist | 20 | 32 | 22 |
| Diffuse | 18 | 17 | 26 |
| Total | 100 | 100 | 100 |
| N = | (61) | (77) | (115) |
| *Attended College* | | | |
| Religious optimist | 8 | 27 | 10 |
| Hopeful | 30 | 19 | 16 |
| Secular optimist | 16 | 0 | 16 |
| Pessimist | 30 | 35 | 42 |
| Diffuse | 16 | 19 | 16 |
| Total | 100 | 100 | 100 |
| N = | (36) | (26) | (31) |

**Table 9.3: Ultimate Value Typology by Catholic School Education for Religious Optimists and Hopefuls with Effect of Level of Education Removed (standard points)**

| Ultimate Value Type | Catholic Grammar and High School | Either Grammar or High School | Neither |
|---|---|---|---|
| Religious optimist | 00 | −14 | −21 |
| Hopeful | 12 | −02 | −16 |

It should also be noted that there are as many pessimists as there are hopefuls among this latter category. One of the side effects of a lot of Catholic schooling appears to be a moderation of pessimism, as well as an addition of hopefulness, since among those with no Catholic education, forty-two percent are pessimists.

Our present data do not enable us to say whether such a finding may represent a particularly strong effect of attendance at a Catholic college, where a more articulate version of Christianity might be learned. Perhaps those who attend the Catholic colleges would know what the "right" answers were on our life situation vignettes. (After all, the answers were made up by two graduates of Catholic colleges!) But whatever the explanation, the fact remains that our evidence does not enable us to dismiss the value-socializing effectiveness of parochial schools. On the contrary, it would seem to us that the issue is now very much an open one.

Finally, the differences in religious optimism and hopefulness (Table 9.3) are not a function of the higher educational attainments of those who had both Catholic grammar school and high

**Table 9.4: Psychological Well-Being by Catholic School Attendance (standard points)**

| | Catholic Grammar and High School | Either Grammar or High School | Neither |
|---|---|---|---|
| *Affect* | | | |
| Positive | 25 | −03 | −06 |
| Negative | 02 | 11 | 02 |
| Balance | 16 | −10 | 02 |
| *Marriage* | | | |
| Positive | 13 | 10 | 00 |
| Negative | −02 | 07 | 17 |
| Balance | 01 | 01 | −10 |

Table 9.5: Psychological Well-Being by Catholic School Attendance with the Effect of Level of Education Removed (standard points)

| | Catholic Grammar and High School | Either Grammar or High School | Neither |
|---|---|---|---|
| *Affect* | | | |
| Positive | 17 | 02 | 00 |
| Negative | 00 | 12 | 00 |
| Balance | 10 | −06 | 02 |
| | | | |
| *Marriage* | | | |
| Positive | 07 | 13 | 04 |
| Negative | 05 | 09 | 19 |
| Balance | 07 | 02 | −09 |

school. Standardizing for the respondent's educational level does not change the findings very much.

If parochial schools produce more religious adults, do they also produce "happier" adults? The data in Table 9.4 somewhat surprisingly suggest that such might be the case. Those who have had both Catholic grammar school and high school are substantially higher on the positive affect score, and somewhat higher on the balance affect score than the other two groups. They are also somewhat above those who did not attend Catholic schools at all in both their positive marriage score and their marriage balance score. While a control for the level of educational attainment (Table 9.5) diminishes the affect differences somewhat, a margin still remains. Indeed, on the marriage balance score the difference is between those who had both Catholic grammar and high school and those who had neither increases from eleven to sixteen standardized points. Higher levels of psychological well-being and marital adjustments are hardly among the claims one hears for parochial school graduates nowadays. Of course, the differences reported in

Table 9.6: Social Attitudes by Attendance at Catholic Schools (standard points)

| | Catholic Grammar and High School | Either Grammar or High School | Neither |
|---|---|---|---|
| Racism | −22 | −09 | −13 |
| Trust | 13 | −14 | −04 |
| Progressive role of women | 00 | −01 | −32 |

Table 9.7: Social Attitudes by Attendance at Catholic Schools with the Effect of the Level of Education Removed (standard points)

| | Catholic Grammar and High School | Either Grammar or High School | Neither |
|---|---|---|---|
| Racism | −07 | −09 | −12 |
| Trust | 01 | −10 | 01 |
| Progressive role of women | −09 | 01 | 00 |

Tables 9.4 and 9.5 are not all that great, but still they will come as a surprise both to the diminishing group of advocates and to the opponents of Catholic parochial education.

Finally, we must inquire whether attendance at parochial school contributes to different social attitudes among Catholics. Table 9.6 seems to indicate that it does. Those who have attended both Catholic grammar school and high school have lower racism scores and higher trust scores than the rest of the Catholic population, and they are right on the mean in attitudes toward the role of women. Those who did not attend Catholic schools at all are thirty-two percent beneath the mean. However these differences, unlike those recorded in previous tables, seem to be to a very considerable extent the result of different levels of educational attainment. Thus, when educational attainment is taken into account (Table 9.7), the racism score of all three groups is virtually the same. And those who went to both Catholic grammar school and high school are eleven points higher on trust than those who went to one or the other, but they score ten points lower in their attitudes toward the role of women. The superior religious sophistication and psychological well-being of those who attended Catholic schools, both at the elementary and secondary level, seems, to a considerable extent, to be independent of the higher educational attainment of the parochial school attenders. But the differences in social attitudes, on the contrary, seem to be accounted for mostly by differences in educational attainment.

## Future Investigations

In this brief chapter, we have taken only a very quick glance at the subject of schools as institutions of the ultimate value socialization. Somewhat to our surprise, we found that such a quick glance, far from closing the question, has opened it wide once again. In further analysis of the data collected in this project, we will have to make a much more careful investigation of the role of the parochial school in value-socialization (although the relatively small number of Catholics will make it difficult for us to do any detailed and precise analysis). *The Education of Catholic Americans* discovered that parochial schools were particularly effective in increasing the level of church attendance among Irish and German Catholics. One wonders if these two ethnic groups are the most susceptible to value-socialization in the schools.

An upcoming replication of *The Education of Catholic Americans* will give us an opportunity to investigate this issue with a much larger number of respondents.[3] It will also, incidentally, represent the second use of our "life situation" approach to ultimate values.

The question of parochial schools has been fraught with emotion in American society for more than a century. It is foolish to suppose that anything as weak as empirical evidence can possibly resolve such a debate. However, empirical evidence can occasionally muddy the waters just a bit, and, rather to our astonishment, we must conclude that the evidence presented in this chapter should have a fair capability of stirring up mud in the murky waters of the question of value education.

# NOTES

1. Daniel P. Moynihan, *Coping: On the Practice of Government,* New York: Random House, 1973.

2. Andrew M. Greeley and Peter H. Rossi, *The Education of Catholic Americans,* Chicago: Aldine, 1966.

3. Andrew M. Greeley, et al., op. cit. (forthcoming).

# Chapter 10

# THE GENERATION GAP?

Since NORC (following the good example of the U.S. Congress) has expanded its national sample to include eighteen-year olds, a number of adolescents did fall into our main sample. In the chapter on mystical experiences, data were presented for a certain rather small number of adolescents, presumably most of them eighteen and nineteen years old. However, in all sample households where there was an adolescent child, a questionnaire was left for that child and for the parent who was not interviewed to fill out. Data were obtained in this fashion for some two hundred teenagers.[1]

In this chapter, we are interested in a limited question, "Is there a religious 'generation gap?' " To answer this question, we will compare the adolescent respondents as a group with our adult respondents as a group. Thus, the comparison is between those adolescent children in our sample households and a representative sample of American adults. Such differences as we may find will not necessarily prove that our adolescent respondents are different from their parents, but merely that they are different from the total adult population.

Most serious sociological research has found relatively little evidence of the so-called generation gap. Furthermore, as we noted earlier in this book, where differences are found one does not know whether we are dealing with *life cycle* changes (teenagers are different from their parents, but they are not different from what their parents were when they were teenagers), a *generational* change (this generation of teenagers is different from what their parents were in the teen years and will be different from their parents on the same variables when they are at the age their parents are now), or *secular* changes (not only are teenagers different from their parents at the same age, but their difference is part of a long-range trend that represents change in the human condition).

The question of life cycle versus generation versus secular trend can only be answered when two kinds of research take place:

(1) longitudinal research, which measures the age group going through the various phases of the life cycle, and

(2) replication research, which asks teenagers five years, ten years, or twenty years from now the same questions that are asked of teenagers today.[2]

One may guess that some of the changes in sexual attitudes (which, incidentally, do not seem to imply changes in sexual behavior) currently taking place in American society do not seem to be life cycle changes. In addition to being generational change, they may also represent a long-range secular trend. On the other hand, the history of human sexual behavior suggests that there may be great cycles moving from puritanism to libertinism and back. Thus, when we are told that contemporary America is sexually permissive, we must ask: "Permissive relative to what? The England of the Regency or the Restoration? The Paris of the Louis'? The Rome of the Caesars or the Borgias? Or even puritan New England, with its practice of 'bundling?' "

In other words, those who claim to see in data which compare young people with their elders a long-range secular trend have been gifted with a special revelation. Since no predecessor of NORC was conducting sample surveys in Rome or Paris or London at the times specified, the sober observer remains skeptical about all "trends," "revolutions," and other widely heralded transformations. If teenagers are deemed more religious and/or less religious than their predecessors, one may well have a "generation gap," but not necessarily much else. One will by no means have an infallible prediction of what the world will be like in ten, twenty, fifty, or a hundred years.

In the first six tables in this chapter, we ask the most basic possible question: "Do teenagers respond differently to the life situation vignettes than do the adults?"

First of all, as might be expected, the adolescents had a harder time answering the questions than did the adults. On only one of the questions, the drafting of a son, were more than fifteen percent of the adults unable to respond (in all likelihood because many of them did not have sons of draft age). On the other hand, between a fifty and a third of the adolescent respondents could not give one of the six precoded answers. Perhaps they had not had any close experience of such life situations, and perhaps they had not yet articulated to themselves a world view which could enable them to respond to such situations when they do occur. However, their pattern of responses is still quite similar to that of the previous generation. For example, both adults and adolescents are most likely to respond with resignation when told of an incurable illness (Table 10.1). On the other hand (Table 10.2), young people are more likely to take a hopeful viewpoint (twenty-four

**Table 10.1: Response to Incurable Disease Question by Generation[a] (in percentages)**

| Statement | Adults | Adolescents |
|---|---|---|
| a)  It will all work out for the best somehow | 13 | 6 |
| b)  No one should question the goodness of God's decision about death | 14 | 9 |
| c)  There is nothing I can do about it so I will continue as before | 39 | 26 |
| d)  I am angry and bitter at this twist of fate | 4 | 6 |
| e)  I have had a full life and am thankful for that | 10 | 14 |
| f)  Death is painful, but it is not the end of me | 5 | 5 |
| g)  I cannot answer this question | 10 | 15 |
| h)  None of the above | 4 | 17 |

a. Question thirteen of the belief systems questionnaire: "You have just visited your doctor and he told you that you have less than a year to live. He has also told you that your disease is incurable. Which of the following statements comes closest to expressing your reaction?"   (CIRCLE ONE)

**Table 10.2: Response to Draft Question by Generation[a] (in percentages)**

| Statement | Adults | Adolescents |
|---|---|---|
| a) Somehow it will all work out | 14 | 9 |
| b) If God wants it to happen it must be all right | 16 | 7 |
| c) This happens to lots of people, you learn to accept it | 22 | 13 |
| d) The lottery system is unjust since it does not take individual situations into consideration | 3 | 5 |
| e) He has been a good brother, and we are thankful for that | 7 | 6 |
| f) It is terrible, but God may provide some opportunity for him to grow and expand his life | 18 | 24 |
| g) I cannot answer this question | 9 | 12 |
| h) None of the above | 9 | 24 |

a. Question fourteen of the belief systems questionnaire: "Your brother is very likely to be drafted and will be going into a dangerous combat area soon. Which of the following statements reflect your reaction?"   (CIRCLE ONE)

percent as opposed to eighteen percent) when presented with the prospect of a brother being drafted. Perhaps it is easier to be hopeful about a brother than about a son.

**Table 10.3: Response to Promotion Question by Generation[a] (in percentages)**

| Statement | Adults | Adolescents |
|---|---|---|
| a) Good things usually happen to those who wait their turn | 17 | 11 |
| b) God has been good to me and my family | 28 | 17 |
| c) These things can go either way, this time it was good | 18 | 17 |
| d) This is a surprise and I am going to enjoy it | 10 | 9 |
| e) I am grateful to my boss for the promotion | 11 | 15 |
| f) This is a good thing, but my religion tells me life would have been OK without the promotion | 7 | 6 |
| g) I cannot answer this question | 5 | 11 |
| h) None of the above | 1 | 11 |

a. Question fifteen of the belief systems questionnaire: "You and your husband or wife have been expecting word of a promotion for several weeks. One day it comes through. Which of the following best reflects your reaction to this good news?"   (CIRCLE ONE)

## Table 10.4: Response to Parent's Dying Question by Generation[a] (in percentages)

| Statement | Adults | Adolescents |
|---|---|---|
| a) They are in pain now, but they will be peaceful soon | 18 | 12 |
| b) Everything that happens is God's will and cannot be bad | 21 | 15 |
| c) There is nothing to do but wait for the end | 5 | 5 |
| d) This waiting is inhuman for them, I hope it ends soon | 13 | 13 |
| e) We can at least be thankful for the good life we have had together | 20 | 24 |
| f) This is tragic, but death is not the ultimate end for us | 13 | 9 |
| g) I cannot answer this question | 7 | 11 |
| h) None of the above | 3 | 10 |

a. Question sixteen of the belief systems questionnaire: "Imagine that one of your parents is dying a slow and painful death and try to figure out for yourself if there is anything that will enable you to understand the meaning of such a tragedy. Which, if any, of the following statements best expresses your state of mind in this situation?" (CIRCLE ONE)

## Table 10.5: Response to Retarded Child Question by Generation[a] (in percentages)

| Statement | Adults | Adolescents |
|---|---|---|
| a) We will try to take care of this child, but it may have to be put in an institution; either way it will all work out | 17 | 11 |
| b) God had His own reasons for sending this child to us | 19 | 7 |
| c) We must learn to accept this situation | 16 | 20 |
| d) I love the baby, but why me? | 3 | 2 |
| e) I'm just plain glad to have the child here | 3 | 11 |
| f) God has sent us a heavy cross to bear and a special child to love | 20 | 26 |
| g) I cannot answer this question | 10 | 17 |
| h) None of the above | 2 | 5 |

a. Question seventeen of the belief systems questionnaire: "Imaging that you have just had a child and that the doctor has informed you that it will be mentally retarded. Which of the following responses comes closest to your own feelings about this situation?" (CIRCLE ONE)

The pattern of the response of the two groups to promotion is virtually the same. The adolescents are a little bit more likely to be grateful to the boss for their promotion and a little less likely to invoke the direct intervention of the diety. They are also less likely to be religiously optimistic on the death of the parent, and more likely to respond with gratitude for the life together that has already been enjoyed (Table 10.4).

Surprisingly enough, the adolescents are more hopeful when faced with the thought of a mentally retarded child and less likely to make either a religious or a secular optimistic response to this life situation. They are also more likely to be fatalists in the face of natural disaster, and (given the number of nonrespondents) more likely to respond more hopefully to such disastrous situations (Table 10.6).

In summary, an inspection of the distribution of the responses of our adult sample and of the adolescent children in sample households would indicate a basic similarity in the two generations

**Table 10.6: Response to Natural Disasters Question by Generation[a]**
**(in percentages)**

| Statement | Adults | Adolescents |
|---|---|---|
| a) We can never really understand these things, but they usually have some unexpected good effect | 5 | 3 |
| b) We cannot know the reasons, but God knows them | 23 | 9 |
| c) We cannot know why these occur and we have to learn to live with that fact | 24 | 28 |
| d) The government is responsible for seeing that these disasters do as little harm as possible | 3 | 5 |
| e) I am grateful that I don't live in a hurricane area | 10 | 9 |
| f) I am not able to explain why these things happen, but I still believe in God's love | 25 | 25 |
| g) I cannot answer this question | 5 | 12 |
| h) None of the above | 4 | 9 |

a. Question eighteen of the basic belief systems questionnaire: "Almost every year hurricanes level homes, flood towns, destroy property, and take human lives. How can we make any sense out of such disasters which happen, apparently, by chance?" (CIRCLE ONE) in reaction to life crisis situations. The adolescents are somewhat less likely to fall back on religious optimism and somewhat more likely to be hopeful in the cases of a retarded child, a natural disaster, and a loved one being drafted. The generation gap, if there is one, seems to indicate a more sophisticated approach to questions of good and evil among adolescents, but there is no more evidence of a massive swing among adolescents to a more pessimistic world view than is to be found in the adult generation.

While the life situation questions indicate little in the way of a generation gap, the religious opinion items (Table 10.7) seem to indicate a substantial gap. Adolescents are similar in their responses only on three items: the rejection of death ending personal existence, the assertion that life would be worthwhile even if death were the absolute end, and the belief that God encourages humans to develop all potential abilities. On many of the items, the differences between adults and adolescents are higher than twenty percentage points.

It is possible that the phenomenon we are dealing with is not so much a rejection of religious convictions of the previous generation as a lack of strong certainty about them. It may be that when the "strongly agree" and the "agree somewhat" (or the "disagree strongly" and the "disagree somewhat") were combined, adolescents and adults might be more like one another in their religious opinions. An inspection of the tabulations shows that such, indeed, seems to be the case. For example (Table 10.8), three-quarters of both adults and adolescents reject the assertion that God's love is not involved in anything that happens in this life, and almost three-fifths of both groups are willing to agree that death may contain a pleasant surprise. There is only a small difference (eighty-five percent and seventy-eight percent) in the proportion thinking that everything in life has a purpose. Nine-tenths of the adults think it is important for their children to believe in God, as do eight-tenths of the adolescents. Eighty-four percent of the adults believe in God and seventy-two percent of the adolescents do, though there the difference is more in the proportion who say they "can't decide."

There are two possible interpretations of the phenomenon presented in Table 10.7 and Table 10.8. It may be that adolescents will simply be less certain people religiously through their whole

Table 10.7: Religious Opinion Items by Generation (in percentages)

| Statement | Adults | Adolescents |
|---|---|---|
| A. Sometimes I am not sure there is any purpose in my life | 68 | 47 |
| B. Whatever happens after death the person that I am will not exist any more[a] | 37 | 36 |
| C. God's goodness and love are greater than we can possibly imagine[b] | 74 | 62 |
| D. Despite all the things that go wrong, the world is still moved by love[b] | 58 | 44 |
| E. God's love is not involved in anything that happens in this life[c] | 57 | 50 |
| F. When faced with a tragic event I try to remember that God still loves me and that there is hope for the future[b] | 68 | 46 |
| G. I feel that it is important for my children to believe in God[b] | 80 | 61 |
| H. I would be happy to be alive even if death were the absolute end[b] | 65 | 64 |
| I. There is more good in the world than bad[b] | 54 | 31 |
| J. God encourages me to develop all of my potential abilities[b] | 52 | 54 |
| K. God is passionately in love with me[b] | 36 | 20 |
| L. The best way to live is to take the daily problems as they come and not worry too much about the big questions of life and death[b] | 58 | 44 |
| M. There may be a God and there may not be[a] | 62 | 37 |
| N. I believe in the existence of God as I define Him[b] | 68 | 47 |
| O. I think that everything that happens has a purpose[b] | 61 | 47 |
| P. Sometimes I look forward to death because life is hard[c] | 64 | 50 |
| Q. I am not sure what I believe[c] | 55 | 33 |
| R. Death may contain a pleasant surprise for us[b] | 35 | 19 |

a. Disagree.
b. Agree strongly.
c. Disagree strongly.

Table 10.8: Agree (or Disagree) "Strongly" or "Somewhat" on Selected
Religious Opinion Items by Generation (in percentages)

| Statement | Adults | Adolescents |
|---|---|---|
| God's love is not involved in anything that happens in this life | 74 | 73 |
| I feel that it is important for my children to believe in God | 91 | 79 |
| I believe in the existence of God as I define Him | 34 | 72 |
| I think that everything that happens has a purpose | 85 | 78 |
| Death may contain a pleasant surprise for us | 59 | 57 |

lives (a generational explanation), or it may be that adolescence is
a time of religious hesitation, uncertainty, and exploration; hence,
a time when one is just less disposed to agree strongly with religious propositions. Only research that traces today's adolescents
through further developmental stages in their life cycles will enable
us to test this possibility. However, there is one reason for inclining
to the life cycle explanation. The response to the life situation
vignettes indicates, if anything, that the adolescent generation is
somewhat more hopeful than its predecessors. It is certainly not
one that is more pessimistic. The lower proportions expressing
strong religious opinions and the higher proportions unable to
respond to the vignette questions seem likely to be signs of inex-
perience, uncertainty, and hesitation.

Confirmation for this explanation can be found in Table 10.9.
There is little difference between adolescents and adults in the
proportion responding positively that man survives after death,
that God's love is behind everything that happens, and that the
universe is not governed by chance. They are somewhat less likely
than their predecessors to think that meaning can be found in
suffering and injustice, and that their prayers are heard. Still,
seven-tenths of the adolescents agree with the former proposition,
and eight-tenths with the latter. However, when one looks at the
second set of columns in Table 10.9, one notes that much smaller
proportions of the teenagers are likely to say that they are "very
sure" about these religious propositions. They agree, then, with
fundamental Western religious beliefs, but they are less certain in
their agreement than are adults.

Table 10.9: Religious Attitudes by Generation (in percentages)

| | "Yes" | | "Very Sure" | |
| | | Adoles- | | Adoles- |
| Statement | Adult | cent | Adult | cent |
|---|---|---|---|---|
| Man survives after death | 61 | 64 | 32 | 25 |
| Universe is not governed by chance | 53 | 56 | 28 | 21 |
| God's love is behind everything that happens | 67 | 63 | 39 | 24 |
| Meaning can be found in suffering and injustice | 78 | 69 | 39 | 29 |
| Prayers are heard | 88 | 79 | 56 | 41 |

That the teen years are times of uncertainty, problems, and confusion is almost universally accepted in American society, even though some authors have pointed out that adolescence as a phase in the life cycle is almost entirely a creation of the American middle class in the present century. Our adult respondents are much less likely to describe themselves as having high life satisfactions when they were teens (a little less than half put themselves on the top three rungs of the ladder), while seven-tenths put themselves on the top three rungs of the ladder "at the present time" (Table 10.10). Interestingly enough, adolescents seem to agree; only fifty-three percent describe themselves as on the top three rungs of the life satisfaction ladder. They are eight percentage points less likely to describe themselves as "very happy."[3] Whether their uncertainty about fundamental issues is linked to their lower levels of personal well-being is a pertinent question for further analysis.

Our teenage respondents are also less likely to think that people can be trusted (Table 10.11). Thus, only one-third of them are

Table 10.10: Psychological Well-Being by Generation (in percentages)

| Statement | Adults | Adolescents |
|---|---|---|
| High life satisfaction as teenager | 47 | 53[a] |
| High life satisfaction now | 70 | 53[a] |
| "Very happy" | 27 | 19 |

a. Same item.

Table 10.11: Social Attitudes by Generation (in percentages)

| Statement | Adults | Adolescents |
|---|---|---|
| Whites have a right to keep blacks out of their neighborhood | 70 | 47 |
| People can be trusted | 49 | 33 |
| Higher income for wife means troubles for the marriage | 44 | 32 |

willing to extend trust to other people, while almost half the older generation are. On the other hand, they are much less likely than the adults to think that whites have the right to try to keep blacks out of their neighborhoods. They are also somewhat less likely than adults to think that the wife being the "breadwinner" will precipitate a marriage crisis. Our adolescent respondents, then, are more enlightened on racial and feminist questions, but more suspicious of others than adults.

Any research project that discovers a generation gap is guaranteed quick media coverage. If young people are different from their parents, particularly if they are dramatically different, this is news of capital importance, because it will either frighten or threaten adults and encourage young people in their conviction that they are not only young but also making a new beginning. Unfortunately for the media possibilities of this report, we can make no claim to have discovered a substantial generation gap. On the contrary, in world views (as measured by the life situation questions), religious opinion, and acceptance of basic religious beliefs, there are very few differences between adolescents and adults. If there is a generation gap at all, it is a "certainty gap." Adults are more certain about their religious convictions. This difference in certainty may well be both a cause and an effect of the generally troubled, suspicious, and confused period that adolescence seems to be in American society.

If there is any difference in ultimate values between adolescents and adults, it would seem that adults are more likely to be religious optimists and adolescents more likely to be hopeful. Such a change, should it be sustained throughout their lives, does not suggest a turning away from religion as it may indicate a somewhat more nuanced and sophisticated response to the problem of good and evil in the world.

The appropriate issue, then, for further research with these data and other data to be collected is not generational difference but generational continuity. Despite all the ferment and unrest in American society, it would seem that the American adult population has been able to transmit its ultimate value systems to the new generation. How this is done, why it is not done in some cases, why it is done better in still other cases, and, finally, why the younger generation may be turning away from naive religious optimism to more sophisticated religious hope strikes us as being far more critical questions than those raised by Margaret Mead, for example, in her *Culture and Commitment*.[4] She argues that the younger generation has its values placed in the future and not in the past. It is doubtful, then, that we encountered very many of Mead's young people in our sample.

## NOTES

1. The "do-it-yourself" questionnaire that was left for the teenager and the other parent was necessarily much shorter than the main survey. The items to be reported in this chapter constitute virtually all these instruments.

2. Ideally, longitudinal and replication research would be combined, and two or more age groups would be followed through phases of the life cycle—clearly a task requiring several generations of social researchers.

3. See item 2 in Appendix A. This item has often been used by Bradburn and others as a substitute for the more elaborate psychological well-being scales.

4. Margaret Mead, *Culture and Commitment*, New York: Doubleday, 1970, (Natural History Press).

*Chapter 11*

# SUMMARY AND CONCLUSION

We began this book with the assumption that religion is not church attendance, ritual observance, doctrinal code, denominational affiliation, or propositional orthodoxy. Religion is, on the contrary, a human's definition of the Real, an interpretative scheme, a primal cultural system, ultimate values, answers to questions of injustice, suffering, surprise, life, and death. Our effort has necessarily been a preliminary one. This is the first time the techniques of national sample survey research have been used to study such ultimate values, and this monograph is but a preliminary summary of our findings after a year and one-half's work. The best we can expect from such a project is that it demonstrate the usefulness of our approach to religion.

## Principal Findings

Our principal findings are as follows:

(1) It is possible to develop survey instruments that measure ultimate values. The responses to our life situation questions fall into theoretically predictable patterns and correlate with demographic, familial, religious, and attitudinal variables in interpret-

able patterns. The life situation questions are surely subject to improvement. We hope that in the years ahead we can improve them ourselves; but, as an approach to measuring ultimate reality, they seem to represent a promising beginning.

(2) On the typology developed from our scales, the religious optimists tend to be female, older rather than younger, black, and from the South. They are also poorer, not so well educated, and Protestant. The hopefuls are somewhat younger, slightly better educated, and also more likely to be Protestant or Irish Catholic. The secular optimists are more frequently British or German Protestants, college-educated, and from the Northeast. Pessimists are overrepresented among the young, among those with college educations, and among Irish Catholics and Jews. The diffuse are more likely to be Italian Catholic or Jewish, and to live in either the Midwest or the Northeast.

(3) The religious behavior of the parents of our respondents and the structure of their family life had an influence on the shaping of ultimate values. Those from more religious families and from families where relationships were perceived as closer were more likely to be religious optimists. Those from less religious and less intimate families were more likely to be pessimists. The pessimists were also less likely to see *anyone* influencing their religious development—pro or con. It also seemed that one's parents' education was more important in shaping one's world view than one's own education.

(4) The religious optimists are the most likely to be "religious" in the traditional fashion, pessimists most likely to be "nonreligious." They are also the most likely to see every human action as religious. The hopefuls, however, are somewhat more likely than religious optimists to be certain of survival after death and to think of themselves as close to God.

(5) The "quality of life" as measured by life satisfaction, psychological well-being and marital adjustment is affected by ultimate values, with the pessimists being much less satisfied with life than the average and the hopefuls much more satisfied with the quality of their lives than the average. To the question of whether religion makes for greater happiness in life, we must answer that it depends on your religion. If you are a religious optimist, it apparently does not. But if you are hopeful, then it does. To the

extent that traditional religions are able to move from an unsophisticated optimism to a hopefulness which accepts evil but does not yield to it, they may produce even more happy people.

(6) Ultimate values do have a moderate effect on social and ethical attitudes, with the religious optimists generally being more "conservative," and the pessimists more "liberal." This difference diminishes but does not disappear when the level of education is taken into account. However, the influences of ultimate values on social attitudes is "filtered through" the educational background and the regional location of the respondents. Only the hopefuls—who are more "liberal" than the optimists, even when education is taken into account—are consistently less likely to be racist. They also have the highest score on trust.

(7) Intense religious experiences are far more common in our society than has been generally realized. The people who have these experiences are neither drug addicts nor psychological misfits; they seem to be less prejudiced and to enjoy a higher level of psychological well-being than other Americans. The father's religious behavior is a strong predictor of such experiences, particularly the joyfulness of his religious style. Basic values, such as religious optimism and hopefulness, seem to be the intervening variables that link the father's religious style with mystical experience. The quality of the mystical experience and the triggers which initiate it are also affected by ultimate values. The hopefuls experience a much more "passionate" kind of ecstasy than the religious optimists.

(8) We could find little evidence of a generation gap between our adult respondents and the teenagers living in our sample households. In both ultimate values and religious opinions, the adolescents seem to be distributed in the same general patterns, although they report much less confidence and certainty about their religious positions than do adult respondents. If there is any difference in ultimate values between adults and teenagers, it is that the latter seem to be less religiously optimistic and more hopeful. The angry pessimism noted in those in their twenties and thirties is *not* reflected in our adolescents.

(9) Parochial schools have a rather notable effect on the ultimate values of those who attend them, with more than two-fifths of college-educated Catholics falling into the hopeful category.

Parochial school Catholics are more likely to report psychological well-being and satisfactory marriages. They are also more likely to have low scores on racism and higher scores on trust. To a greater extent than we had believed possible, it would appear that the school can be an important institution of socialization in ultimate values.

## Future Research

In the course of this monograph, we have noted a number of paths to be explored in greater detail as we continue the analysis of the data on which this work is based. Among the principal tasks remaining in the analysis of these data are the following:

(1) The explanatory models presented briefly must be elaborated, developed, and modified.

(2) Of capital importance is the analysis of the family units—mother-father-adolescent, about which we have information. Such analysis will enable us to answer critical questions about the transmission of ultimate values across generational lines.

(3) We must study further the religious impact of paranormal experiences, which both are more widespread in American society and have greater impact than we have hitherto realized.

(4) Our explanatory models must be tested not only for the whold population but for the major subgroups within the population as well. In particular, questions must be raised as to whether the explanatory models apply within the various denominational (and perhaps ethnic) categories.

At the present time, four further projects are planned:

(1) A study of the causal models of ultimate values.

(2) A report on religious socialization and the transmission of religious attitudes, values, and behaviors across generational lines.

(3) A more intensive study of paranormal experiences.

(4) A popular book, that discusses, especially for religious professionals, the practical implications of our findings for ordinary religious life.

In the course of this book we have remarked frequently on the need for further research. (Indeed, it would be false to the customs of the social science fraternity were we not to do so.)

(1) Our life situation vignettes must be improved and refined, and then administered to large subpopulations—religious, ethnic, regional groups, and especially high school and college students.

(2) This study should be replicated periodically to see if there is any change in the ultimate values of the American population with the passage of time.

(3) Even though it is extremely expensive, there is no substitute for longitudinal research for following an age group through the various developmental phases of the life cycle, particularly adolescence, youth, and early marriage. Only then can our causal models be subjected to the rigorous tests required for them to stand as proven.

(4) The mechanics and dynamics of socialization in ultimate values in the family environment ought to be studied with much more precise and detailed observation of what occurs in the family situation.

(5) The influence of the school in ultimate value socialization must also be studied. As we have remarked already, the forthcoming replication of the NORC study of the education of Catholic Americans should provide a partial opportunity to explore this area.

(6) It would be helpful if those who are studying aging and death could measure the relationship between ultimate values, as we have defined them, and the response of men and women to death, not as an abstract question but as an impending reality.

(7) The relationship between ultimate values and ethical and social attitudes and behavior, explored very tentatively in this study, ought to be examined in much greater detail.

(8) Much more attention should be paid to the impact of the paranormal on human life, and especially to mystical ecstasy, which seems to have a strong, positive contribution to make to life satisfaction and psychological well-being.

This study has been an attempt to break from a tradition of sociological inquiry that seems to us to have been relatively unfruitful. In our judgment, there is little point in asking whether people are getting less religious (or more religious), especially when there are no data from the past to enable us to make comparisons. A far more pertinent issue is what people may think of the ultimate order of things. And if one asks this question, one must also ask what are the origins of these ultimate values, and what impact do such values have on the rest of their lives?

Before we can address ourselves to such questions, it is necessary to obtain a theoretically predictable and substantively interpretable measure of ultimate values. We believe that we have made a beginning in that direction, so that it is indeed possible to measure with survey instruments the ultimate values of a population. As we predicted, such values are rooted in economic and demographic characteristics, family environment, childhood and teenage religiousness, and intense religious experiences in later life. As we further predicted, these values in turn affected confidence in survival, psychological well-being, trust of other humans, racial attitudes, and even the nature of mystical experiences, for those who had them.

We have made only a beginning in what we hope is a new course for research on religion. It is an incomplete beginning; how adequate it is, is for others to say. Still, it *is* a beginning.

And the "Malek Yahweh" had better watch Himself, because before we are finished we may just try to administer an NORC questionnaire to Him. We may even be able to get Him on a log linear model.

November, 1972

# NATIONAL OPINION RESEARCH CENTER
University of Chicago

## INTERVIEW SCHEDULE

## APPENDIX A

<table>
<tr><td>TIME BEGAN:</td><td>_____ AM<br>PM</td></tr>
</table>

1. We are interested in the way people are feeling these days. During the past few weeks, did you ever feel--

BEGIN DECK 01

| | | Yes | No | |
|---|---|---|---|---|
| A. | Particularly excited or interested in something? | 1 | 2 | 10/9 |
| B. | Did you ever feel so restless that you couldn't sit still long? | 3 | 4 | 11/9 |
| C. | Proud because someone complimented you on something you had done? | 5 | 6 | 12/9 |
| D. | Very lonely or remote from other people? | 7 | 8 | 13/9 |
| E. | Pleased about having accomplished something? | 1 | 2 | 14/9 |
| F. | Bored? | 3 | 4 | 15/9 |
| G. | On top of the world? | 5 | 6 | 16/9 |
| H. | Depressed or very unhappy? | 7 | 8 | 17/9 |
| I. | That things were going your way? | 1 | 2 | 18/9 |
| J. | Upset because someone criticized you? | 3 | 4 | 19/9 |

2. Taken altogether, how would you say things are these days--would you say that you are very happy, pretty happy, or not too happy?

Very happy . . . . 1     20/9

Pretty happy . . . 2

Not too happy . . . 3

3. Here are some statements about which people have different opinions. Would you tell me your opinion on each one?

| CARD A | Agree strongly | Agree slightly | Can't decide | Disagree slightly | Disagree strongly | Don't know/ Can't answer | |
|---|---|---|---|---|---|---|---|
| A. People can be divided into two distinct classes: the weak and the strong. | 1 | 2 | 3 | 4 | 5 | 6 | 21/9 |
| B. Strong discipline builds moral character. | 1 | 2 | 3 | 4 | 5 | 6 | 22/9 |
| C. There is hardly anything lower than a person who does not feel a great deal of love, gratitude, and respect for his or her parents. | 1 | 2 | 3 | 4 | 5 | 6 | 23/9 |
| D. Faith in the super- natural is a harmful self-delusion. | 1 | 2 | 3 | 4 | 5 | 6 | 24/9 |

3. Continued

| | Agree strongly | Agree slightly | Can't decide | Disagree slightly | Disagree strongly | Don't know/ Can't answer |
|---|---|---|---|---|---|---|
| E. Sex crimes, like rape and child-molesting, are caused by a sick society instead of guilty individuals. | 1 | 2 | 3 | 4 | 5 | 6  25/9 |
| F. To be a decent human being, follow your conscience regardless of the law. | 1 | 2 | 3 | 4 | 5 | 6  26/9 |
| G. Negroes shouldn't push themselves where they are not wanted. | 1 | 2 | 3 | 4 | 5 | 6  27/9 |
| H. White people have the right to keep Negroes out of their neighborhoods if they want to, and Negroes ought to respect that right. | 1 | 2 | 3 | 4 | 5 | 6  28/9 |

ASK WHITE RESPONDENTS ONLY:

4. How strongly would you object if a member of your family wanted to bring a Negro friend home to dinner?

Not at all strongly . . . 1    29/9
Somewhat strongly . . . . 2
Very strongly . . . . . . 3
Don't know . . . . . . . 4

ASK EVERYONE:

5. Do you think white students and Negro students should go to the same schools, or to separate schools?

Same schools . . . . . . . 1    30/9
Separate schools . . . . . 2
Don't know . . . . . . . . 3

6. Do you think most people would try to take advantage of you if they got the chance or would they try to be fair?

Would take advantage . . . 1    31/9
Would be fair . . . . . . 2
Don't know . . . . . . . . 3

7. Would you say that most of the time people to be helpful or that they are mostly just looking out for themselves?

$$\begin{array}{ll} \text{Try to be helpful} \quad . \quad . \quad . \quad . \quad 1 & 32/9 \\ \text{Look out for themselves} \quad . \quad 2 & \\ \text{Don't know} . \quad . \quad . \quad . \quad . \quad . \quad 3 & \end{array}$$

8. Generally speaking, would you say that most people can be trusted or that you can't be too careful in dealing with people?

$$\begin{array}{ll} \text{Most can be trusted} \quad . \quad . \quad . \quad 1 & 33/9 \\ \text{Can't be too careful} \quad . \quad . \quad . \quad 2 & \\ \text{Don't know} . \quad . \quad . \quad . \quad . \quad . \quad 3 & \end{array}$$

9. Are you currently--married, widowed, divorced, separated, or have you never been married?

$$\begin{array}{ll} \text{Married} \quad . \quad . \quad . \quad . \quad . \quad 1 & 34/9 \\ \text{Widowed} \quad . \quad . \quad . \quad . \quad . \quad 2 & \\ \text{Divorced} \quad . \quad . \quad . \quad . \quad 3 & \\ \text{Separated} \quad . \quad . \quad . \quad . \quad 4 & \\ \text{Never married} \quad . \quad . \quad 5 & \end{array}$$

10. Now I am going to read some items concerning personal attitudes and traits. For each one, please tell me whether you think the item is _true_ for you or _false_ for you.

|   |   | True | False |   |
|---|---|---|---|---|
| A. | I have never intensely disliked anyone . . . . . . . . | 1 | 2 | 35/9 |
| B. | When I see a child crying, I usually stop and comfort him . . . . . . . . . . . . . . . . . . . . . . . . . | 3 | 4 | 36/9 |
| C. | I sometimes feel resentful when I don't get my way . . . | 5 | 6 | 37/9 |
| D. | I like to gossip at times . . . . . . . . . . . . . . | 1 | 2 | 38/9 |
| E. | No matter whom I'm talking to, I'm always a good listener | 3 | 4 | 39/9 |
| F. | I don't find it particularly difficult to get along with loud-mouthed, obnoxious people . . . . . . . . . . . . | 5 | 6 | 40/9 |
| G. | There have been occasions when I felt like smashing things . . . . . . . . . . . . . . . . . . . . . . . . | 1 | 2 | 41/9 |

11. Now, a different question.  Please tell me whether or not you think it should be possible for a pregnant woman to obtain a <u>legal</u> abortion if . . . READ EACH STATEMENT, AND CIRCLE ONE CODE FOR EACH.

| | Yes | No | Don't know | |
|---|---|---|---|---|
| If there is a strong chance of serious defect in the baby? . . . . . . . . . . | 1 | 2 | 3 | 42/9 |
| If she is married and does not want any more children? . . . . . . . . . . . . | 4 | 5 | 6 | 43/9 |

12. There's been a lot of discussion about the way morals and attitudes about sex are changing in this country.  For example--a man and a woman having sex relations before marriage--do you think that is always wrong, almost always wrong, wrong only sometimes, or not wrong at all?

|  |  |
|---|---|
| Always wrong . . . . . . . 1 | 44/9 |
| Almost always wrong . . . 2 | |
| Wrong only sometimes . . . 3 | |
| Not wrong at all . . . . . 4 | |
| Don't know . . . . . . . 5 | |

13. For each of the following statements I am going to read now, give me the answer that best describes your agreement or disagreement.

| CARD A | Agree strongly | Agree slightly | Can't decide | Disagree slightly | Disagree strongly | Don't know/ Can't answer | |
|---|---|---|---|---|---|---|---|
| A. A pre-school child is likely to suffer emotional damage if his mother works. | 1 | 2 | 3 | 4 | 5 | 6 | 45/9 |
| B. A wife should respond to her husband's sexual overtures even when she is not interested. | 1 | 2 | 3 | 4 | 5 | 6 | 46/9 |
| C. If a wife earns more money than her husband, the marriage is headed for trouble. | 1 | 2 | 3 | 4 | 5 | 6 | 47/9 |
| D. A husband should respond to his wife's sexual overtures even when he is not interested. | 1 | 2 | 3 | 4 | 5 | 6 | 48/9 |
| E. Parents should encourage just as much independence in their daughters as in their sons. | 1 | 2 | 3 | 4 | 5 | 6 | 49/9 |

14.  Please look at the circle on this card.  The rings are meant to represent how
     close or how far you may feel in certain kinds of relationships.  The inside

| CARD B |

     ring--1--stands for "very close."  Outside the circle--6--stands for "not at
     all close."  The other rings stand for different degrees of closeness in
     between.  For each relationship I am going to ask you about, please tell me
     which numbered ring best represents how close you feel.

 A.  How close do you feel to God most of the time?  (Which number in the circle?)
     CIRCLE ONE CODE.

        1         2         3         4         5         6

                                                Can't answer . . . . . 7      50/9

 B.  How close do you feel to your church most of the time?  CIRCLE ONE CODE.

        1         2         3         4         5         6

                                                Can't answer . . . . . 7      51/9

                                                Doesn't apply to me;
                                                have no church . . . 8

 C.  IF CURRENTLY MARRIED:  How close do you feel to your (husband/wife) most
                            of the time?  CIRCLE ONE CODE.

        1         2         3         4         5         6

                                                Can't answer . . . . . 7      52/9

                                                                             53/R

15.  This next question is about you and your family during the time you were growing
     up.  Most families contain a number of "twosomes"; such as you and your mother,
     your father and your mother, and so on.

 A.  The first twosome is your father and
     your mother--would you say that, dur-        Very close . . . . . . 1      54/9
     ing the time you were growing up, they       Somewhat close . . . . 2
     were very close to each other, some-         Not at all close . . . 3
     what close, or not at all close?

 B.  How about you and your mother--during
     the time that you were growing up           Very close . . . . . . 1      55/9
     were you very close to each other,           Somewhat close . . . . 2
     somewhat close, or not at all close?         Not at all close . . . 3

 C.  And you and your father--during the
     time that you were growing up were          Very close . . . . . . 1      56/9
     you very close to each other, somewhat       Somewhat close . . . . 2
     close, or not at all close?                  Not at all close . . . 3

 D.  And how strict was your father with
     you when you were growing up--very          Very strict . . . . . 1      57/9
     strict, somewhat strict, or not at          Somewhat strict . . . 2
     all strict?                                 Not at all strict . . 3

 E.  How strict was your mother with you--
     very strict, somewhat strict, or not        Very strict . . . . . 1      58/9
     at all strict?                              Somewhat strict . . . 2
                                                 Not at all strict . . 3

BEGIN DECK 02

16. Now I am going to read you some experiences that can influence a person's religious outlook, either toward religion or away from it. Please tell me, for each one, how important that was in influencing your <u>own present</u> feelings about religion--very important, somewhat important, or not at all important?

| | | Very important | Somewhat important | Not at all important | |
|---|---|---|---|---|---|
| A. | Your parents' religious behavior. | 1 | 2 | 3 | 10/9 |
| B. | Things your parents told you about God. | 1 | 2 | 3 | 11/9 |
| C. | Religious education in school. | 1 | 2 | 3 | 12/9 |
| D. | Your father's way of living. | 1 | 2 | 3 | 13/9 |
| E. | Your mother's way of living. | 1 | 2 | 3 | 14/9 |
| F. | Friends when you were in high school. | 1 | 2 | 3 | 15/9 |
| G. | Friends after high school. | 1 | 2 | 3 | 16/9 |
| H. | IF EVER MARRIED: Your (husband/wife). | 1 | 2 | 3 | 17/9 |
| I. | Priests, ministers, rabbis, etc. | 1 | 2 | 3 | 18/9 |
| J. | Some book(s) you have read. | 1 | 2 | 3 | 19/9 |
| K. | General atmosphere in which you were raised. | 1 | 2 | 3 | 20/9 |

17. We are also interested in the kinds of activities people think of as "religious." For each of the activities I am going to mention now, please tell me which category best describes it, according to <u>your own definition</u> of "religious."

| CARD C | | Definitely religious | Probably religious | Probably not religious | Certainly not religious | Can't answer | |
|---|---|---|---|---|---|---|---|
| A. | Thanking God for a promotion. | 1 | 2 | 3 | 4 | 5 | 21/9 |
| B. | Giving money to the poor. | 1 | 2 | 3 | 4 | 5 | 22/9 |
| C. | Going to Church services. | 1 | 2 | 3 | 4 | 5 | 23/9 |
| D. | Visiting a sick friend. | 1 | 2 | 3 | 4 | 5 | 24/9 |
| E. | Making love. | 1 | 2 | 3 | 4 | 5 | 25/9 |
| F. | Eating dinner with friends. | 1 | 2 | 3 | 4 | 5 | 26/9 |
| G. | Demonstrating against the war. | 1 | 2 | 3 | 4 | 5 | 27/9 |
| H. | Listening to beautiful music. | 1 | 2 | 3 | 4 | 5 | 28/9 |

IF RESPONDENT IS CURRENTLY MARRIED, ASK Q'S. 18 AND 19.　OTHERS SKIP TO Q. 20.

18. I'm going to read you some things that married couples often do together.　Tell me which ones you and your (husband/wife) have done together <u>in the past few weeks</u>.

| | | Yes | No | |
|---|---|---|---|---|
| A. | Visited friends together. | 1 | 2 | 29/9 |
| B. | Gone out together to a movie, bowling, sporting events of some kind or some other entertainment. | 1 | 2 | 30/9 |
| C. | Spent an evening just chatting with each other. | 1 | 2 | 31/9 |
| D. | Ate out in a restaurant together. | 1 | 2 | 32/9 |
| E. | Entertained friends in your home. | 1 | 2 | 33/9 |
| F. | Had a good laugh together or shared a joke. | 1 | 2 | 34/9 |
| G. | Taken a drive or gone for a walk just for pleasure. | 1 | 2 | 35/9 |
| H. | Did something that the other one particularly appreciated. | 1 | 2 | 36/9 |
| I. | Been affectionate toward each other. | 1 | 2 | 37/9 |

19. Now I am going to read you some things about which husbands and wives sometimes agree and sometimes disagree.　Would you tell me, for each one, whether or not it caused a difference of opinion between you, or was a problem in your marriage, <u>during the past few weeks</u>.

| | | Yes | No | |
|---|---|---|---|---|
| A. | Time spent with friends. | 1 | 2 | 38/9 |
| B. | Household expenses. | 1 | 2 | 39/9 |
| C. | Being tired. | 1 | 2 | 40/9 |
| D. | Being away from home too much. | 1 | 2 | 41/9 |
| E. | In-laws. | 1 | 2 | 42/9 |
| F. | Not showing love. | 1 | 2 | 43/9 |
| G. | Your (or your [SPOUSE'S]) job. | 1 | 2 | 44/9 |
| H. | How to spend leisure time. | 1 | 2 | 45/9 |
| I. | Irritating personal habits. | 1 | 2 | 46/9 |

<u>ASK EVERYONE</u>:

20. All of us want certain things out of life.  Think about what really matters in
your own life; what your hopes and wishes are for the future; what your life has
been like in the past.  The figure on this card represents the "ladder of life."
The top rung--10--represents the <u>best that your life could be</u>.  The bottom rung--
0--represents the <u>worst that it could be</u>.  Please tell me the number of the rung
that represents . . . READ CATEGORIES AND CODE FOR EACH.

| CARD D | | | | | | | | | | | | | |
|---|---|---|---|---|---|---|---|---|---|---|---|---|---|
| A. | Where you were as a child. | 00 | 01 | 02 | 03 | 04 | 05 | 06 | 07 | 08 | 09 | 10 | 47-48/99 |
| B. | Where you were as an adolescent (teenager). | 00 | 01 | 02 | 03 | 04 | 05 | 06 | 07 | 08 | 09 | 10 | 49-50/99 |
| C. | Where you are right now. | 00 | 01 | 02 | 03 | 04 | 05 | 06 | 07 | 08 | 09 | 10 | 51-52/99 |
| D. | Where you think you will be five years from now. | 00 | 01 | 02 | 03 | 04 | 05 | 06 | 07 | 08 | 09 | 10 | 53-54/99 |

21. Using the same ladder, try to think of the <u>most religious</u> you think you could be
and make that the top rung--10.  Now think of the <u>least religious</u> you could be
and make that the bottom of the ladder--0.  Now, please tell me the number of the
rung that represents . . . READ CATEGORIES AND CODE FOR EACH.

| CARD D | | | | | | | | | | | | | |
|---|---|---|---|---|---|---|---|---|---|---|---|---|---|
| A. | Where you were as a child. | 00 | 01 | 02 | 03 | 04 | 05 | 06 | 07 | 08 | 09 | 10 | 55-56/99 |
| B. | Where you were as an adolescent (teenager). | 00 | 01 | 02 | 03 | 04 | 05 | 06 | 07 | 08 | 09 | 10 | 57-58/99 |
| C. | Where you are right now. | 00 | 01 | 02 | 03 | 04 | 05 | 06 | 07 | 08 | 09 | 10 | 59-60/99 |
| D. | Where you think you will be five years from now. | 00 | 01 | 02 | 03 | 04 | 05 | 06 | 07 | 08 | 09 | 10 | 61-62/99 |

63-67/R

22. On this sheet of paper are some statements about the deeper meaning of life and man's thoughts about the ultimate purpose of living. For each one, please circle the number under the answer that best describes how you feel about that statement. HAND YELLOW SHEET AND PENCIL TO RESPONDENT.  IF R. CANNOT OR DOES NOT WISH TO SELF-ADMINISTER THIS, YOU MAY READ THE ITEMS.  DO NOT CODE IN THE QUESTIONNAIRE; CODE ON YELLOW SHEET ONLY.

|     |  | Agree strongly | Agree somewhat | Can't decide | Disagree somewhat | Disagree strongly | |
| --- | --- | --- | --- | --- | --- | --- | --- |
| A. | Sometimes I am not sure there is any purpose in my life. | 1 | 2 | 3 | 4 | 5 | 10/9 |
| B. | Whatever happens after death the person that I am now will not exist any more. | 1 | 2 | 3 | 4 | 5 | 11/9 |
| C. | God's goodness and love are greater than we can possibly imagine. | 1 | 2 | 3 | 4 | 5 | 12/9 |
| D. | Despite all the things that go wrong, the world is still moved by love. | 1 | 2 | 3 | 4 | 5 | 13/9 |
| E. | God's love is not involved in anything that happens to us in this life. | 1 | 2 | 3 | 4 | 5 | 14/9 |
| F. | When faced with a tragic event I try to remember that God still loves me and that there is hope for the future. | 1 | 2 | 3 | 4 | 5 | 15/9 |
| G. | I feel that it is important for my children to believe in God. | 1 | 2 | 3. | 4 | 5 | 16/9 |
| H. | I would be happy to be alive even if death were the absolute end. | 1 | 2 | 3 | 4 | 5 | 17/9 |
| I. | There is more good in the world than bad. | 1 | 2 | 3 | 4 | 5 | 18/9 |
| J. | God encourages me to develop all of my potential abilities. | 1 | 2 | 3 | 4 | 5 | 19/9 |
| K. | God is passionately in love with me. | 1 | 2 | 3 | 4 | 5 | 20/9 |
| L. | The best way to live is to take the daily problems as they come and not worry too much about the big questions of life and death. | 1 | 2 | 3 | 4 | 5 | 21/9 |
| M. | There may be a God and there may not be. | 1 | 2 | 3 | 4 | 5 | 22/9 |
| N. | I believe in the existence of God as I define Him. | 1 | 2 | 3 | 4 | 5 | 23/9 |
| O. | I think that everything that happens has a purpose. | 1 | 2 | 3 | 4 | 5 | 24/9 |
| P. | Sometimes I look forward to death because life is hard. | 1 | 2 | 3 | 4 | 5 | 25/9 |
| Q. | I am not sure what I believe. | 1 | 2 | 3 | 4 | 5 | 26/9 |
| R. | Death may contain a pleasant surprise for us. | 1 | 2 | 3 | 4 | 5 | 27/9 |

CIRCLE ONE: ⟶    R. self-administered . . . . 1    28/9
Interviewer read items . . . 2
Combination . . . . . . . . 3

23. Now I am going to read you some statements about which people often express
different opinions.  Please tell me how you feel about each one.

A.  Man survives after death.

| | |
|---|---|
| Yes . [ASK (1)] . . 1 | 29/9 |
| No . (GO TO B) . . 2 | |

   (1)  IF YES:  How sure are you about this?  READ CATEGORIES.

| | |
|---|---|
| Very sure . . . . . 1 | 30/9 |
| Pretty sure . . . . 2 | |
| Not too sure . . . 3 | |

B.  God's love is behind everything that happens.

| | |
|---|---|
| Yes . [ASK (1)] . . 1 | 31/9 |
| No . (GO TO C) . . 2 | |

   (1)  IF YES:  How sure are you about this?  READ CATEGORIES.

| | |
|---|---|
| Very sure . . . . . 1 | 32/9 |
| Pretty sure . . . . 2 | |
| Not too sure . . . 3 | |

C.  The universe is not governed by chance.

| | |
|---|---|
| Yes . [ASK (1)] . . 1 | 33/9 |
| No . (GO TO D) . . 2 | |

   (1)  IF YES:  How sure are you about this?  READ CATEGORIES.

| | |
|---|---|
| Very sure . . . . . 1 | 34/9 |
| Pretty sure . . . . 2 | |
| Not too sure . . . 3 | |

D.  Meaning can be found in suffering and in injustice.

| | |
|---|---|
| Yes . [ASK (1)] . . 1 | 35/9 |
| No . (GO TO E) . . 2 | |

   (1)  IF YES:  How sure are you about this?  READ CATEGORIES.

| | |
|---|---|
| Very sure . . . . . 1 | 36/9 |
| Pretty sure . . . . 2 | |
| Not too sure . . . 3 | |

E.  My prayers are heard.

| | |
|---|---|
| Yes . [ASK (1)] . . 1 | 37/9 |
| No . . . . . . . . 2 | |

   (1)  IF YES:  How sure are you about this?  READ CATEGORIES.

| | |
|---|---|
| Very sure . . . . . 1 | 38/9 |
| Pretty sure . . . . 2 | |
| Not too sure . . . 3 | |

Now I am going to describe some situations to you. These are things that happen to people sometimes, and I want you to _imagine_ that they are happening to you. Please tell me which response on the card comes closest to your own feelings.

24. You have just visited your doctor and he has told you that you have less than a year to live. He has also told you that your disease is incurable. Which of the following statements comes closest to expressing your reaction?

CARD
E

   a) It will all work out for the best somehow . . . . . . . . . . 1       39/9

   b) No one should question the goodness of God's decision about
      death . . . . . . . . . . . . . . . . . . . . . . . . . . . . 2

   c) There is nothing I can do about it so I will continue as
      before . . . . . . . . . . . . . . . . . . . . . . . . . . . 3

   d) I am angry and bitter at this twist of fate . . . . . . . . . 4

   e) I have had a full life and am thankful for that . . . . . . . 5

   f) Death is painful, but it is not the end of me . . . . . . . . 6

   g) I cannot answer this question . . . . . . . . . . . . . . . . 7

   h) None of the above . . . . . . . . . . . . . . . . . . . . . . 8

---

25. Your son is very likely to be drafted and will be going into a dangerous combat area soon. Which of the following statements reflect your reaction?

CARD
F

   a) Somehow it will all work out . . . . . . . . . . . . . . . . . 1       40/9

   b) If God wants it to happen it must be all right . . . . . . . . 2

   c) This happens to lots of people, you learn to accept it . . . . . 3

   d) The lottery system is unjust since it does not take individual
      situations into consideration . . . . . . . . . . . . . . . . 4

   e) He has been a good son and we are thankful for that . . . . . . 5

   f) It is terrible, but God may provide some opportunity for him
      to grow and expand his life . . . . . . . . . . . . . . . . . 6

   g) I cannot answer this question . . . . . . . . . . . . . . . . 7

   h) None of the above . . . . . . . . . . . . . . . . . . . . . . 8

26.  You and your husband or wife have been expecting word of a promotion for several
     weeks.  One day it comes through.  Which of the following best reflects your
     reaction to this good news?

CARD
G

   a)  Good things usually happen to those who wait their turn  . . . . 1      41/9

   b)  God had been good to me and my family . . . . . . . . . . . . 2

   c)  These things can go either way, this time it was good  . . . . . 3

   d)  This is a surprise and I am going to enjoy it  . . . . . . . . 4

   e)  I am grateful to my boss for the promotion . . . . . . . . . . 5

   f)  This is a good thing, but my religion tells me life would have
        been OK without the promotion  . . . . . . . . . . . . . . . 6

   g)  I cannot answer this question  . . . . . . . . . . . . . . . 7

   h)  None of the above . . . . . . . . . . . . . . . . . . . . . . 8

27.  Imagine that one of your parents is dying a slow and painful death and try to
     figure out for yourself if there is anything that will enable you to understand
     the meaning of such a tragedy.  Which, if any, of the following statements best
     expresses your state of mind in this situation?

CARD
H

   a)  They are in pain now, but they will be peaceful soon . . . . . . 1      42/9

   b)  Everything that happens is God's will and cannot be bad  . . . . 2

   c)  There is nothing to do but wait for the end . . . . . . . . . 3

   d)  This waiting is inhuman for them,  I hope it ends soon . . . . . 4

   e)  We can at least be thankful for the good life we have had
        together . . . . . . . . . . . . . . . . . . . . . . . . . . 5

   f)  This is tragic, but death is not the ultimate end for us . . . . 6

   g)  I cannot answer this question . . . . . . . . . . . . . . . . 7

   h)  None of the above . . . . . . . . . . . . . . . . . . . . . . 8

28. Imagine that you have just had a child and that the doctor has informed you that it will be mentally retarded. Which of the following responses comes closest to your own feelings about this situation?

CARD
I

    a) We will try to take care of this child, but it may have to be put in an institution; either way it will all work out . . . . 1     43/9

    b) God had his own reasons for sending this child to us . . . . . . 2

    c) We must learn to accept this situation . . . . . . . . . . . 3

    d) I love the baby, but why me? . . . . . . . . . . . . . . . . 4

    e) I'm just plain glad to have the child here . . . . . . . . . . 5

    f) God has sent us a heavy cross to bear and a special child to love . . . . . . . . . . . . . . . . . . . . . . . . . . . . 6

    g) I cannot answer this question . . . . . . . . . . . . . . . 7

    h) None of the above . . . . . . . . . . . . . . . . . . . . . 8

---

29. Almost every year hurricanes level homes, flood towns, destroy property, and take human lives. How can we make any sense out of such disasters which happen, apparently, by chance? Which of the following statements best describes your answer?

CARD
J

    a) We can never really understand these things, but they usually have some unexpected good effect . . . . . . . . . . . . . . . 1     44/9

    b) We cannot know the reasons, but God knows them . . . . . . . . 2

    c) We cannot know why these occur and we have to learn to live with that fact . . . . . . . . . . . . . . . . . . . . . . . . 3

    d) The government is responsible for seeing that these disasters do as little harm as possible . . . . . . . . . . . . . . . . 4

    e) I am grateful that I don't live in a hurricane area . . . . . . 5

    f) I am not able to explain why these things happen, but I still believe in God's love . . . . . . . . . . . . . . . . . . . 6

    g) I cannot answer this question . . . . . . . . . . . . . . . 7

    h) None of the above . . . . . . . . . . . . . . . . . . . . . 8

30. Now to something very different. How often have you had any of the following
    experiences?  READ EACH ITEM AND CIRCLE ONE CODE FOR EACH.

| CARD K | | Never in my life | Once or twice | Several times | Often | I cannot answer this question | |
|---|---|---|---|---|---|---|---|
| A. | Thought you were somewhere you had been before, but knowing that it was impossible. | 1 | 2 | 3 | 4 | 5 | 45/9 |
| B. | Felt as though you were in touch with someone when they were far away from you. | 1 | 2 | 3 | 4 | 5 | 46/9 |
| C. | Seen events that happened at a great distance as they were happening. | 1 | 2 | 3 | 4 | 5 | 47/9 |
| D. | Felt as though you were really in touch with someone who had died. | 1 | 2 | 3 | 4 | 5 | 48/9 |
| E. | Felt as though you were very close to a powerful, spiritual force that seemed to lift you out of yourself? | 1 | 2 | 3 | 4 | 5 | 49/9 |

[ASK (1) - (3)]

(1)  IF RESPONDENT ANSWERED CATEGORIES 2, 3, or 4 TO "E":

CARD L

Many people who have had such experiences say that there are "triggers"
or specific events or circumstances that set them off.  Have any on
this card ever started such an experience for you?  Just give me the
number of the ones that have.  CODE AS MANY AS APPLY.

| | | | |
|---|---|---|---|
| a) | The beauties of nature such as a sunset . . . . . . . . . | 1 | 50/9 |
| b) | Watching little children . . . . . . . . . . . . . . . | 2 | 51/9 |
| c) | Child birth . . . . . . . . . . . . . . . . . . . . . | 3 | 52/9 |
| d) | Prayer . . . . . . . . . . . . . . . . . . . . . . . | 4 | 53/9 |
| e) | Reading the Bible . . . . . . . . . . . . . . . . . | 5 | 54/9 |
| f) | Listening to a sermon . . . . . . . . . . . . . . . | 6 | 55/9 |
| g) | Sexual lovemaking . . . . . . . . . . . . . . . . . | 7 | 56/9 |
| h) | Your own creative work . . . . . . . . . . . . . . . | 1 | 57/9 |
| i) | Looking at a painting . . . . . . . . . . . . . . . | 2 | 58/9 |
| j) | Being alone in Church . . . . . . . . . . . . . . . | 3 | 59/9 |
| k) | Listening to music . . . . . . . . . . . . . . . . . | 4 | 60/9 |
| l) | Reading a poem or a novel . . . . . . . . . . . . . | 5 | 61/9 |
| m) | Moments of quiet reflection . . . . . . . . . . . . | 6 | 62/9 |
| n) | Attending a church service . . . . . . . . . . . . . | 7 | 63/9 |
| o) | Physical exercise . . . . . . . . . . . . . . . . . | 1 | 64/9 |
| p) | Something else (PLEASE DESCRIBE) . . . . . . . . . . | 2 | 65/9 |

q)  Have there been other things, like drugs, which started the
    experience for you?  RECORD VERBATIM.

30.  Continued

(2)  Those who have had these kinds of experiences have given various descriptions of what they were like.  Here is a list of some of the things they say happen.  Have any of them ever happened to you during any of your experiences?  CODE AS MANY AS APPLY.

CARD
M

    a)  A feeling of a new life or of living in a new world . . . 1     10/9

    b)  A sense of the unity of everything and my own part in it  2     11/9

    c)  An experience of great emotional intensity . . . . . . 3     12/9

    d)  A great increase in my understanding of knowledge . . . . 4     13/9

    e)  A feeling of deep and profound peace . . . . . . . . . 5     14/9

    f)  Sense that all the universe is alive . . . . . . . . . 6     15/9

    g)  Sense of joy and laughter . . . . . . . . . . . . . . 7     16/9

    h)  Sense of my own need to contribute to others . . . . . . 1     17/9

    i)  A feeling of desolation . . . . . . . . . . . . . . . . 2     18/9

    j)  A sensation of warmth or fire . . . . . . . . . . . . `. . . 3     19/9

    k)  A sense that I was being bathed in light . . . . . . . 4     20/9

    l)  A loss of concern about worldly problems . . . . . . . 5     21/9

    m)  A feeling that I couldn't possibly describe what was
        happening to me . . . . . . . . . . . . . . . . . . 6     22/9

    n)  The sensation that my personality has been taken over
        by something much more powerful than I am . . . . . . 7     23/9

    o)  A sense of being alone . . . . . . . . . . . . . . . 1     24/9

    p)  A certainty that all things would work out for the good . 2     25/9

    q)  A confidence in my own personal survival . . . . . . . 3     26/9

    r)  A sense of tremendous personal expansion, either psycho-
        logical or physical . . . . . . . . . . . . . . . . . 4     27/9

    s)  A conviction that love is at the center of everything . . 5     28/9

    t)  Something else (PLEASE DESCRIBE) . . . . . . . . . . . 6     29/9

---

(3)  Approximately how long did your experience(s) (average time if more than one) last?

                         A few minutes or less . . 1     30/9

                         Ten or fifteen minutes . . 2

                         Half an hour . . . . . . 3

                         An hour . . . . . . . . 4

                         Several hours . . . . . 5

                         A day or more . . . . . 6

31.  What is your religious preference?  Is it Protestant, Catholic, Jewish, some other
religion, or no religion?

        Protestant (ASK A) . 1       Other  (SPECIFY RELIGION AND/OR    31/9
        Catholic . (ASK B) . 2       CHURCH AND DENOMINATION)
        Jewish . . . . . . . 3
        None . . . . . . . . 4       _____ 5

A.  IF PROTESTANT:  What specific denomination is that, if any?

        Baptist . . . . . . 1       Other (SPECIFY) _____    32/9
        Methodist . . . . . 2
        Lutheran . . . . . 3       _____ 6
        Presbyterian . . . . 4       No denomination given or non-
        Episcopalian . . . . 5       denominational church . . . 7

B.  IF CATHOLIC:

|  |  | Yes | No |  |
|---|---|---|---|---|
| (1) | Did you ever attend public elementary schools? . . . . | 1 | 2 | 33/9 |
| (2) | Did you ever attend Catholic elementary schools? . . . | 1 | 2 | 34/9 |
| (3) | Did you ever attend public high schools? . . . . . . . | 1 | 2 | 35/9 |
| (4) | Did you ever attend Catholic high schools? . . . . . . | 1 | 2 | 36/9 |

32.  IF CURRENTLY MARRIED:  What is your (husband's/wife's) religious preference?

        Protestant (ASK A) . 1       Other (SPECIFY RELIGION AND/OR    37/9
        Catholic . . . . . . 2       CHURCH AND DENOMINATION)
        Jewish . . . . . . . 3
        None . . . . . . . . 4       _____ 5

A.  IF PROTESTANT:  What specific denomination is that, if any?

        Baptist . . . . . . 1       Other (SPECIFY) _____    38/9
        Methodist . . . . . 2
        Lutheran . . . . . 3       _____ 6
        Presbyterian . . . . 4       No denomination given or non-
        Episcopalian . . . . 5       denominational church . . . 7

33.  What was your father's (father substitute's) religious preference at the time
you were growing up?

        Protestant (ASK A) . 1       Other (SPECIFY RELIGION AND/OR    39/9
        Catholic . . . . . . 2       CHURCH AND DENOMINATION)
        Jewish . . . . . . . 3
        None . . . . . . . . 4       _____ 5

A.  IF PROTESTANT:  What specific denomination is that, if any?

        Baptist . . . . . . 1       Other (SPECIFY) _____    40/9
        Methodist . . . . . 2
        Lutheran . . . . . . 3       _____ 6
        Presbyterian . . . . 4       No denomination given or non-
        Episcopalian . . . . 5       denominational church . . . 7

34. What was your mother's (mother substitute's) religious preference at the time you were growing up?

| Protestant (ASK A) . 1 | Other (SPECIFY RELIGION AND/OR | 41/9 |
|---|---|---|
| Catholic . . . . . . 2 | CHURCH AND DENOMINATION) | |
| Jewish . . . . . . . 3 | | |
| None . . . . . . . . 4 | _____ 5 | |

A. IF PROTESTANT: What specific denomination is that, if any?

| Baptist. . . . . . . 1 | Other (SPECIFY) _____ | 42/9 |
|---|---|---|
| Methodist . . . . . 2 | | |
| Lutheran . . . . . . 3 | _____ 6 | |
| Presbyterian . . . . 4 | No denomination given or non- | |
| Episcopalian . . . . 5 | denominational church . . . 7 | |

35.

|  | Very joyous | Somewhat joyous | Not at all joyous | Not religious | |
|---|---|---|---|---|---|
| A. When you were growing up, how would you describe your father's personal approach to religion? | 1 | 2 | 3 | 4 | 43/9 |
| B. How about your mother's personal approach to religion, how would you describe it? | 1 | 2 | 3 | 4 | 44/9 |

36.

|  | Several times a week | Every week | Nearly every week | 2-3 times a month | About once a month | Several times a year | About once or twice a year | less than once a year | Never | |
|---|---|---|---|---|---|---|---|---|---|---|
| A. How often do you attend religious services? USE CATEGORIES AS PROBES, IF NECESSARY. | 01 | 02 | 03 | 04 | 05 | 06 | 07 | 08 | 09 | 45-46 99 |
| B. IF CURRENTLY MARRIED: How often does your (husband/wife) attend religious services? | 01 | 02 | 03 | 04 | 05 | 06 | 07 | 08 | 09 | 47-48 99 |
| C. When you were growing up, how often did your father (father substitute) attend religious services? | 01 | 02 | 03 | 04 | 05 | 06 | 07 | 08 | 09 | 49-50 99 |
| D. When you were growing up, how often did your mother (mother substitute) attend religious services? | 01 | 02 | 03 | 04 | 05 | 06 | 07 | 08 | 09 | 51-52 99 |

37.  About how often do you pray?

Several times a day  . . . 1        53/
Once a day . . . . . . . . 2
Several times a week . . . 3
Once a week . . . . . . . 4
Less than once a week . . 5

ASK FOR EACH--A-D:

38.  How far did (you/PERSON) go in school?  (Regular school for which you/PERSON got credits toward a diploma or a degree.)  USE CATEGORIES AS PROBES, IF NECESSARY. PROBE FOR BEST GUESS.

|  | 8th grade or less | Some high school | High school graduate | Some college | College graduate | Graduate or professional degree beyond the bachelor's | Don't know | |
|---|---|---|---|---|---|---|---|---|
| A. How far did you ... | 1 | 2 | 3 | 4 | 5 | 6 | 7 | 54/ |
| B. IF CURRENTLY MARRIED: Your (husband/wife) ... | 1 | 2 | 3 | 4 | 5 | 6 | 7 | 55/ |
| C. Your father (father substitute) ... | 1 | 2 | 3 | 4 | 5 | 6 | 7 | 56/ |
| D. Your mother (mother substitute) ... | 1 | 2 | 3 | 4 | 5 | 6 | 7 | 57/ |

39.  How many of your grandparents were born in the United States?

None . . . . . 0        58/
One  . . . . . 1
Two  . . . . . 2
Three  . . . . 3
Four  . . . . 4
Don't know . . 5

40. From what countries or part of the world did your ancestors come?

IF SINGLE COUNTRY IS NAMED, REFER TO NATIONAL
CODE BELOW, AND ENTER CODE NUMBERS IN BOXES:

IF MORE THAN ONE COUNTRY IS NAMED, ENTER
CODE 88 AND ASK A.

. . . . . . . ☐☐     10-11
                     99

A. IF MORE THAN ONE COUNTRY NAMED: Which one of these countries do you feel
closer to?

IF ONE COUNTRY NAMED, REFER TO
CODES BELOW, AND ENTER CODE NUMBER HERE:

IF CAN'T DECIDE ON ONE COUNTRY, ENTER CODE 88.

. . . . . ☐☐     12-13
                 99

### NATIONAL CODES

| | | | |
|---|---|---|---|
| Africa | 01 | Mexico | 17 |
| Austria | 02 | Netherlands (Dutch/Holland) | 18 |
| Canada (French) | 03 | Norway | 19 |
| Canada (Other) | 04 | Philippines | 20 |
| China | 05 | Poland | 21 |
| Czechoslovakia | 06 | Puerto Rico | 22 |
| Denmark | 07 | Russia (USSR) | 23 |
| England and Wales | 08 | Scotland | 24 |
| Finland | 09 | Spain | 25 |
| France | 10 | Sweden | 26 |
| Germany | 11 | Switzerland | 27 |
| Greece | 12 | West Indies | 28 |
| Hungary | 13 | Other (SPECIFY) _____ | |
| Ireland | 14 | _____ | 29 |
| Italy | 15 | More than one country/can't decide on one | 88 |
| Japan | 16 | Don't know | 98 |

41. Generally speaking, do you usually
think of yourself as a Republican,
Democrat, Independent, or what?

Republican . . (ASK A) . 1     14/9
Democrat . . . (ASK A) . 2
Independent . (ASK B) . 3
Other (GO TO Q. 40). . . 4

A. IF REPUBLICAN OR DEMOCRAT: Would you call yourself a strong (Republican/
Democrat) or not a very strong (Republican/
Democrat)?

Strong. . . . (GO TO Q. 40) . 1     15/9
Not very strong (GO TO Q. 40) . 2

B. IF INDEPENDENT: Do you think of yourself as closer to the Republican or
Democratic Party?

Republican . . . 1     16/9
Democratic . . . 2
Neither . . . . . 3

42. Last week were you working full time, part time, going to school, keeping house, or what?

IF MORE THAN ONE RESPONSE, GIVE PREFERENCE TO CODES IN NUMERICAL ORDER--FROM LEAST TO HIGHEST NUMBERS. CIRCLE ONE CODE ONLY.

Working full time (35 hours or more) 1     17/9

Working part time (1 to 34 hours)  . 2

With a job, but not at work because of temporary illness, vacation, strike . . . . . . . . . . . . . 3

Unemployed, laid off, looking for work . . . . . . . . . . . . . 4

Retired . . . (SKIP TO Q. 42) . . . 5

In school . . (SKIP TO Q. 42) . . . 6

Keeping house  (SKIP TO Q. 42) . . . 7

Other (SPECIFY AND SKIP TO Q. 42)

_____ 8

43. A. What kind of work do you normally do? That is, what is your job called?

OCCUPATION: _____

B. IF NOT ALREADY ANSWERED, ASK: What do you actually do in that job? Tell me, what are some your main duties?

18-20/

21-22/

C. What kind of place do you work for?

INDUSTRY: _____

D. IF NOT ALREADY ANSWERED, ASK: What do they (make/do)?

E. IF ALREADY ANSWERED, CODE WITHOUT ASKING: Are you self-employed or do you work for someone else?

Self-employed . . . 1

Someone else  . . . 2

IF RESPONDENT IS CURRENTLY MARRIED, ASK Q. 44.  OTHERS SKIP TO Q. 46.

44.  Last week was your (wife/husband) working full time, part time, going to school, keeping house, or what?

> IF MORE THAN ONE RESPONSE, GIVE PREFERENCE TO CODES IN NUMERICAL ORDER--FROM LEAST TO HIGHEST NUMBERS.  CIRCLE ONE CODE ONLY.
>
> Working full time (35 hours or more) 1          23/9
>
> Working part time (1 to 34 hours)  . 2
>
> With a job, but not at work because temporary illness, vacation, strike . . . . . . . . . . . . . 3
>
> Unemployed, laid off, looking for work . . . . . . . . . . . . . . 4
>
> Retired  . . . (SKIP TO Q. 44) . . . 5
>
> In school  . . (SKIP TO Q. 44) . . . 6
>
> Keeping house  (SKIP TO Q. 44) . . . 7
>
> Other (SPECIFY AND SKIP TO Q. 44)
>
> _____ 8

45.  A.  What kind of work does (SPOUSE) normally do?  That is, what is (his/her) job called?

    OCCUPATION: _____

    B.  IF NOT ALREADY ANSWERED, ASK:  What does (SPOUSE) actually do in that job? Tell me, what are some of (his/her) main duties?

                                                        24-26/

                                                        27-28/

    C.  What kind of place does (SPOUSE) work for?

    INDUSTRY: _____

    D.  IF NOT ALREADY ANSWERED, ASK:  What do they (make/do)?

    E.  IF ALREADY ANSWERED, CODE WITHOUT ASKING:  Is (he/she) self-employed or does (he/she) work for someone else?

                        Self-employed . . . 1

                        Someone else  . . . 2

                        Don't know . . . . 3

DECK 05

ASK EVERYONE:

46. How many members of this household are your own teenaged children, ages 13 through 19?

_____  29/

47. In which of these groups did your total family income, from all sources, fall last year--1971--before taxes, that is?  Just tell me the letter.

<table>
<tr><td rowspan="12">HAND<br>CARD<br>K</td><td>A.</td><td>Under $1,000 . . . . . .</td><td>01</td><td>30-31</td></tr>
<tr><td>B.</td><td>$1,000 to 2,999 . . . . .</td><td>02</td><td>99</td></tr>
<tr><td>C.</td><td>$3,000 to 3,999 . . . . .</td><td>03</td><td></td></tr>
<tr><td>D.</td><td>$4,000 to 4,999 . . . . .</td><td>04</td><td></td></tr>
<tr><td>E.</td><td>$5,000 to 5,999 . . . . .</td><td>05</td><td></td></tr>
<tr><td>F.</td><td>$6,000 to 6,999 . . . . .</td><td>06</td><td></td></tr>
<tr><td>G.</td><td>$7,000 to 7,999 . . . . .</td><td>07</td><td></td></tr>
<tr><td>H.</td><td>$8,000 to 9,999 . . . . .</td><td>08</td><td></td></tr>
<tr><td>I.</td><td>$10,000 to 14,999 . . . .</td><td>09</td><td></td></tr>
<tr><td>J.</td><td>$15,000 to 19,999 . . . .</td><td>10</td><td></td></tr>
<tr><td>K.</td><td>$20,000 to 24,999 . . . .</td><td>11</td><td></td></tr>
<tr><td>L.</td><td>$25,000 or over . . . . .</td><td>12</td><td></td></tr>
</table>

Refused . . . . . . . . . . 13

Don't know . . . . . . . . 98

48. In what year were you born?  [ ][ ][ ][ ]    32-33
99

49. CODE RESPONDENT'S SEX:    Male . . . . . 1    34/
Female . . . . 2

CODE WITHOUT ASKING ONLY IF THERE IS NO DOUBT IN YOUR MIND.

50. What race do you consider yourself?  RECORD VERBATIM AND CODE.

White . . . . 1    35/
Black . . . . 2
Other (SPECIFY

_____ 3

NOTE:  IF YOU ASKED R'S RACE, CHECK BOX . . . [ ]    36/

Thank you very much for your time and help.

51.  May I have your name and telephone number just in case my office wants to verify this interview?

RESPONDENT'S                                    TELEPHONE
NAME: _____           NUMBER: _____

                                                No phone . . . . . . 2   37/9
                                                Refused phone number 3

IF TELEPHONE NUMBER IS GIVEN, ASK A:
A.  Is this phone located in your home?          Yes . . . . . . . . .4
                                                No (SPECIFY WHERE
                                                    PHONE IS LOCATED)5

_____

                          Thank you.

                                                 ┌─────────────────────┐
                                                 │ TIME _____   AM  │
                                                 │ ENDED:          PM  │
                                                 └─────────────────────┘

                    PSU #    SEGMENT #  PAGE #  LINE #

ENTER FROM LISTING SHEET:  [ ][ ][ ]  [ ][ ][ ]  [ ][ ][ ]  [ ][ ][ ]  ←        38-40/
                                                                                41-43/
                                                                                44-45/
                                               ENTER THIS 11-DIGIT NUMBER       46-48/
52.  IF R IS CURRENTLY MARRIED (Q.9), AND/OR   ON SPOUSE AND/OR YOUTH
     IF R'S OWN TEENAGED CHILDREN LIVE IN HOUSEHOLD (Q. 46)  QUESTIONNAIRE(S) BEFORE LEAVING
                                               THEM WITH RESPONDENT.

     EXPLAIN TO RESPONDENT:  I would like to leave (this/these) short questionnaire(s) for your
     [husband/wife/(and) your teenager(s) to fill out.  The letter from our Director on the front
     page explains what our study is about and how the questionnaire should be filled out.

     I will leave an envelope (for each one) to return the questionnaire to our Chicago office.  No
     stamp is needed--just ask your (husband/wife/son/daughter) to drop it in the mailbox as soon as
     possible.  (The number I have put on the back will notify my office that the questionnaire(s)
     are from the correct household.  They will not be associated with your name.)

     CODE (AND ENTER) BELOW WHICH AND HOW MANY "MAIL-BACK" QUESTIONNAIRES YOU HAVE LEFT WITH THIS
     RESPONDENT.

                                                  No      Yes
                        Spouse questionnaire       0       1              49/9
                        Youth questionnaire        0    How many? _____ 50/9

_____

          FILL OUT ITEMS BELOW AS SOON AS POSSIBLE AFTER LEAVING RESPONDENT

A.  Length of Interview _____ minutes   51-53/     D.  Comments about this interview.

B.  Date of Interview  [ ][ ]  [ ][ ]       54-57/
                       MONTH    DAY

C.  In general, what was the respondent's
    attitude toward the interview?
         Friendly and interested . . . . 1           58/9
         Cooperative, but not
             particularly friendly . . . . 2
         Indifferent and bored . . . . . 3

INTERVIEWER SIGNATURE: _____   INTERVIEWER # [ ].[ ][ ][ ]   59-63/

                                                               [ ][ ][ ][ ]   [1]

Factors and Loadings Greater than .199

|  | Faith | Common Sense | Survival | Agnosticism |
|---|---|---|---|---|
| Sometimes I am not sure there is any purpose in my life. | ... | .344 | -.208 | .436 |
| Whatever happens after death the person that I am now will not exist any more. | ... | .373 | ... | ... |
| God's goodness and love are greater than we can possibly imagine. | .728 | ... | ... | ... |
| Despite all the things that go wrong, the world is still moved by love. | .459 | ... | ... | .222 |
| God's love is not involved in anything that happens to us in this life. | .314 | .432 | ... | ... |
| When faced with a tragic event I try to remember that God still loves me and that there is hope for the future. | .843 | ... | ... | ... |
| I feel that it is important for my children to believe in God. | .693 | ... | ... | ... |
| I would be happy to be alive even if death were the absolute end. | ... | .393 | .240 | ... |
| There is more good in the world than bad. | ... | ... | ... | .369 |
| God encourages me to develop all of my potential abilities. | .748 | ... | ... | ... |
| God is passionately in love with me. | .516 | ... | .250 | ... |
| The best way to live is to take the daily problems as they come and not worry too much about the big questions of life and death. | ... | .491 | ... | ... |
| There may be a God and there may not be. | .383 | .471 | ... | ... |
| I believe in the existence of God as I define Him. | .364 | ... | .232 | ... |
| I think that everything that happens has a purpose. | .469 | ... | .283 | .242 |
| Sometimes I look forward to death because life is hard. | ... | ... | .578 | ... |
| I am not sure what I believe. | ... | .416 | ... | .308 |
| Death may contain a pleasant surprise for us. | .257 | ... | .354 | ... |

# APPENDIX B

# CONSTRUCTION OF THE
# ULTIMATE VALUES TYPOLOGY

The typology was constructed from the responses to five vignettes. The original response categories are listed on page 2.7 of this report. There are five stages in the typology construction.

Stage One.   The six original response categories are collapsed into four.

| Old Categories | New Categories |
| --- | --- |
| Religious Optimism | Same |
| Secular Optimism & Grateful Acceptance | Secular Optimism |
| Hopeful | Same |
| Resignation & Anger | Pessimism |

Stage Two.   The responses to the vignettes were then summed for the new categories. A respondent could, for example, have given the hopeful response for none of the vignettes, or for all of them, or for some portion of them.

Stage Three.   Missing data for the vignettes was tabulated and converted into missing data for the typology. If a respondent did not give a useable answer to any of the vignettes they were coded as missing for the typology.

Stage Four.   The summed responses from stage two were collapsed into two categories. Respondents with 0, 1, or 2 were coded as 1 for this stage, and those with 3, 4, or 5 were coded 2. For example, if a person gave the hopeful response to none or one or two of the vignettes, they were now coded as 1 in the Hopeful category of the "new" categories in stage one. If they gave more than two hopeful responses they were coded as a 2.

Stage Five.   The typology of Ultimate Values was computed from the data as it existed after stage four. First of all the four "new" categories were multiplied by successive products of 10. The formula was: (Pessimism x 1) + (Secular Optimism x 10) + (Religious Optimism x 100) + (Hopeful x 1000). This operation then produced the following array.

| Computed Score from Stage Five[a] | N | Label Assigned on Final Typology |
|---|---|---|
| 1111 | 202 | Diffuse |
| 1112 | 380 | Pessimist |
| 1121 | 274 | Secular Optimist |
| 1122 | 73 | Diffuse |
| 1211 | 226 | Religious Optimist |
| 1212 | 22 | Religious Optimist |
| 1221 | 34 | Religious Optimist |
| 2111 | 175 | Hopeful |
| 2112 | 7 | Hopeful |
| 2121 | 33 | Hopeful |
| 2211 | 28 | Hopeful |
| 9999 | 13 | Missing Data |

a. The digits from left to right represent Hopeful, Religious Optimism, Secular Optimism and Pessimism.

# ABOUT THE AUTHORS

WILLIAM C. McCREADY is currently Associate Program Director for the Center for the Study of American Pluralism, and Senior Study Director at the National Opinion Research Center of the University of Chicago. In addition, he is Assistant Professor of Sociology at Loyola University of Chicago, and Managing Editor of the publication *Ethnicity*. Among his other publications are *Report to the Hauser Panel Study of School Segregation in Chicago,* and articles in *Concilium* and in the *National Catholic Reporter.*

ANDREW M. GREELEY is Director of the Center for the Study of American Pluralism and the National Opinion Research Center of the University of Chicago. He is the author of numerous books, among them *Ecstasy: A Way of Knowing* (Prentice-Hall, 1974), *Unsecular Man* (Schocken, 1972), *The Denominational Society* (Scott, Foresman, 1972), and *Religion in the Year 2000* (Sheed & Ward, 1969). His new book, *Ethnicity in the United States: A Preliminary Reconnaissance,* is forthcoming from John Wiley.